HINDU FASTS & FESTIVALS

Suresh Narain Mathur

DIAMOND BOOKS

© Publisher

Published 2007

DIAMOND POCKET BOOKS PVT. LTD.
X-30, Okhla Industrial Area
Phase-2, New Delhi-110020
Phone-011-41611861 Fax-011-41611866
E-mail: sales@diamondpublication.com
www.dpb.in

No part of this publication may be reproduced, stored in a retrieval system, or transmitted, in any form or by any means, electronic, mechanical, photocopying, recording or otherwise, without the prior permission of the publishers.

Cover & Book Design by
ARTEMAS

Picture courtesy:
We are very thankful to
find good images.

Basant Panchami - Sanyal
Holi - Dadsena, Salmonchick
Maker - Amazonas, Malyalam, Gyanf
Bhai Duj - Vishal Raithatha
Cheeti chatt - Jyoti, Avani patel, Arup Dutta
Chhath- eliashama, Kaivant
Shivratri- Srimaitreya
Putradi - mysticreation
Pongal- Anandselvi
Baisakhi- Byte
Bihu- Sanjay Goshwami, Trishikh Das gupta
Durga Puja- Arindam Thokder
Ganesh Chaturthi- Abhinav, Avni Patel, Rahul
Gangaur- Prabhat, Steven Caudill
Ramnavami- Mayapur, Jaywanth kul
Onam- George renju hilup
Sharavani Mela- Kfe
Rakhi- Prodigalsista
Akshya Tritiya- Gopal
Lohri- Gautam Rishi
Vishu- Suresh C Nair
Karva Chauth- Nikhil Dutta, Pravin
Guru Govind- Guru Mastak Singh
Satyanarayan Katha- Bindu Singh, Rathinmamtura
Somvar Vrata- Nagpai
Hindu Costom and Traditionns - Diya, Adlaw, Mayapur
Dussera- G. Athimoolam
Skanda Shasthi- Avni Patel, Byronic
Vaitarni Vrata- Justin Sahib Deen

ISBN- 81-288-1402-8
Price: Rs 495.00

Printed in India by
Best Photo Offset
New Delhi, India

Hinduism -Religion of Multiple Gods 4
Fasts-Their Significance 8
Festivals-Their importance 10
Customs and Traditions - A Prologue 12

Fasts & Festivals
(In chronological order of seasons & in alphabetical order under each season.)

SHISHIR
(Winters/Magh-Phalgun/January-March)

Basant Panchmi 26
Holi Festival 28
Lohri Festival 32
Makar Sankranti 34
Mahashivratri 38
Pongal 44
Vaikunth Ekadashi 46

Contents

VASANT
(Spring/Chaitra-Vaisakh/March- May)
Akshya Tritiya 48
Ashokashthami 51
Baisakhi 52
Bihu 55
Buddha Purnima 59
Chaitra Festival 62
Chaitra Parva 63
Chaitra Purnima 64
Chandan Yatra 65
Cheti Chand 66
Gangaur 69
Gudi Padava 71
Hanuman Jayanti 72
Janaki Navami 74
Mahavir Jayanti 75
Rama Naumi 79
Shankaracharya Jayanti 81
Sheetala Ashtami 82
Ugadi Parva 83
Vishu 85

GREESHMA
(Summers/Jyeshta-Ashadh/May--July)
Guru Purnima 87
Jyaishtha Ashtami 88
Nirjala Ekadashi 89
Rath Yatra 91
Snan Yatra 94
Vata Savitri 95

PAVAS
(Rainy Season/Sawan-Bhadon/July-September)
Anant Chaturdashi 96
Ganesh Chaturthi 97
Haritalika Teej 101
Janmashtami 102
Nag Panchami 105
Onam 108
Putrada Ekadashi 111
Shravani Mela 116
Teej 117
Tirupati Festival 119
Tulsidas Jayanti 120

SHARAD
(Autumn/Ashwin-Kartik/September-November)
Bhaiya Duj 122
Chhath Puja 123
Deepawali 127
Devuthani Ekadashi 130
Dhan Teras 131
Durga Puja 132
Dussehra 141
Govardhan Puja 145
Guru Parab 146
Kartik Purnima 150
Kartik Snan 151
Karwa Chauth 153
Narak Chaturdashi 156
Pitra Paksha 157
Sharad Purnima 158
Skanda Shashthi 159
Surya Shashthi 161
Valmiki Jayanti 162

HEMANT
(Mild Winter/Marg Sheersh- Paush/November -January)
Guru Gobind Singh Jayanti 163
Vaitarani Vrata 165

Other important fasts & festivals
Kumbha Parva 166
Mal-Mas 168
Mangalvar Vrata 169
Pradosha Vrata 170
Satyanarayana Katha 172
Shukravar Vrata 175
Somvar Vrata 176

Reference Information
Vikram Samwat 177
(Months and Days)
Fairs and Festivals of India - A chronological list 179
Glossary-cum-Dictionary 182

Hinduism
Religion of Multiple Gods

Indian subcontinent is the land of mixed culture, colour, caste and creed and is understood to have the oldest civilization of the world. When Christians, Muslims or Jews first encounter Hinduism they are likely to be struck by the profusion of gods and goddesses vividly represented in paintings, sculptures and other art forms – colourful, often sensuous, sometimes humorous. After a visit to India, poet Mark Twain wrote: "India has two million gods, and worship them all. In religion all countries are paupers; India is the only millionaire."

There are three principal deities in Hinduism: Brahma, Vishnu and Mahesh (Shiva), sometimes referred to as the Hindu Trinity. Brahma is thought of as the creator, Vishnu as the sustainer of life and Shiva is associated with dissolution and death.

Yet, first impression can sometimes be mistaken, for many Hindus regard their gods and goddesses as manifestations of the supreme divinity, *Brahman*. In the *Vedantic* schools of Hinduism, *Brahman* is the name given to the concept of the unchanging, infinite, immanent and transcending reality – that is the Divine Ground of All Being. This Supreme Cosmic spirit is regarded to be eternal, genderless, omnipotent, and omniscient.

There are many religions in the world and they usually have a propounder i.e. a person who has started a religion, like the Prophet (Islam), Christ (Christainity), Guru Nanak (Sikhism) and many more, like Mahavir, Buddha, Zarathushtra etc. But Hinduism does not come in that class as it has no single propounder. It has come into existence through time, suiting the lives of the people of the land.

Hinduism is not founded nor propounded by a single man or group of people. It has neither been formulated nor designed in one day or over a lifetime. It grew slowly and gradually through time allowing all the changes and incorporating all new ideals brought in from people pouring down from distant lands.

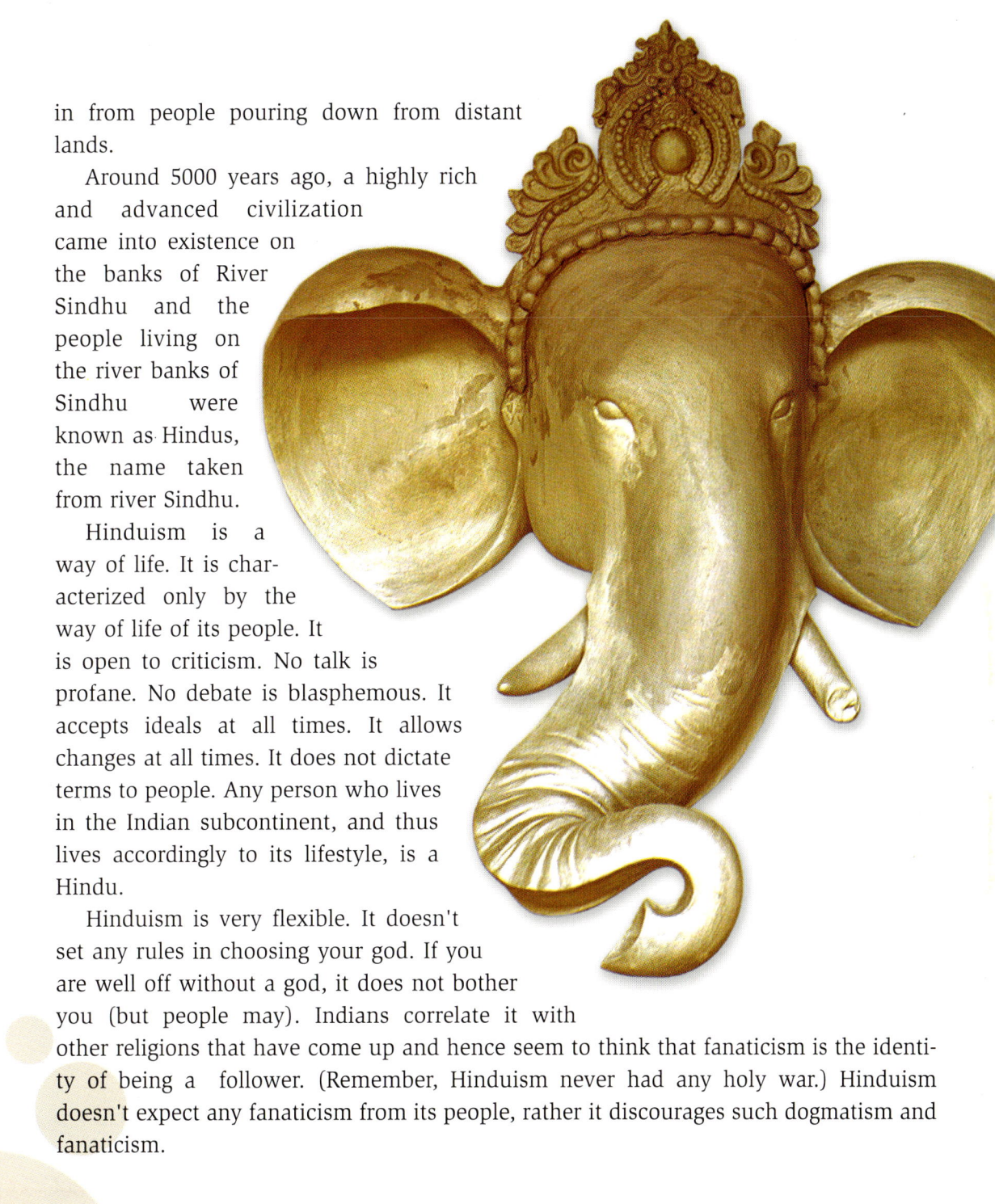

Around 5000 years ago, a highly rich and advanced civilization came into existence on the banks of River Sindhu and the people living on the river banks of Sindhu were known as Hindus, the name taken from river Sindhu.

Hinduism is a way of life. It is characterized only by the way of life of its people. It is open to criticism. No talk is profane. No debate is blasphemous. It accepts ideals at all times. It allows changes at all times. It does not dictate terms to people. Any person who lives in the Indian subcontinent, and thus lives accordingly to its lifestyle, is a Hindu.

Hinduism is very flexible. It doesn't set any rules in choosing your god. If you are well off without a god, it does not bother you (but people may). Indians correlate it with other religions that have come up and hence seem to think that fanaticism is the identity of being a follower. (Remember, Hinduism never had any holy war.) Hinduism doesn't expect any fanaticism from its people, rather it discourages such dogmatism and fanaticism.

What is Hinduism? It is a religion! Not quite right. The most obvious misconception about Hinduism is that we tend to see it as a religion, a faith. Hinduism is a way of life, a *Dharma*. *Dharma* does not mean religion, it is the law that governs all actions. Thus, contrary to popular perception, Hinduism is not a religion. For centuries the world has misinterpreted this, and out of this misinterpretation, have come most of the misconceptions about Hinduism.

Words like Hindu or Hinduism are anachronisms. They do not exist in the Indian cultural lexicon. People have coined them to suit their needs at different points in history. Nowhere in the scriptures is there any reference to Hinduism.

Writings we now categorise as Hindu scriptures include not just books relating to spirituality but also secular pursuits like science, medicine and engineering. This is another reason why it defies classification as a religion. Further, it cannot be claimed to be essentially a school of metaphysics. Nor can it be described as 'otherworldly'. In fact one can almost identify Hinduism with a civilization that is flourishing even now.

The Aryan invasion theory having been completely discredited, it cannot be assumed that Hinduism was the pagan faith of invaders belonging to a race called Aryans. Rather it was the common metafaith of people of various races, including Harappans. The Sanskrit word '*Aryan*' is a word of honourable address, not the racial reference invented by European scholars and put to perverse use by the Nazis.

Evidence that Hinduism must have existed even before circa 10000 B.C. is available. The importance attached to the river Saraswati and the numerous references to it in the *Rigveda* indicates that the *Rigveda* was composed well before 6500 B.C. The first vernal equinox recorded in the *Rigveda* is that of the star Ashwini, which is now known to have occurred around 10000 B.C. Subhash Kak, a computer engineer and a reputed Indologist, 'decoded' the *Rigveda* and found many advanced astronomical concepts therein. The technological sophistication required to even anticipate such concepts is unlikely to have been acquired by a nomadic people, as the invasionists would like us to believe. In his book *"Gods, Sages and Kings"*, David Frawley provides compelling evidence to substantiate this claim.

Many believe that multiplicity of deities makes Hinduism polytheistic. Such a belief is nothing short of mistaking the wood for the trees. The bewildering diversity of Hindu belief – theistic, atheistic and agnostic – rests on a solid unity. "*Ekam sath, vipraah bahudhaa vadanti*", says the *Rigveda* : The Truth (God, *Brahman*, etc) is one, scholars call it by various names. What the multiplicity of deities does indicate is Hinduism's spiritual hospitality as evidenced by two characteristically Hindu doctrines: the doctrine of spiritual competence *(Adhikaara)* and the doctrine of the chosen deity *(Ishhta Devata)*. The doctrine of spiritual competence requires that the spiritual practices prescribed to a person should correspond to his or her spiritual competence. The doctrine of the chosen deity gives a person the freedom to choose (or invent) a form of *Brahman* that satisfies his spiritual cravings and to make it the object of his worship. It is notable that both the doctrines are consistent with Hinduism's assertion that the unchanging reality is present in everything, even in the transient.

Fasts
Their Significance

Fast and eliminate (all filth).
Fast and cleanse.
Fast and revitalize.
Fast and conserve (energy).
Fast and cure (all diseases).
Fast and pray.
Fast and meditate.

Man's foremost duty is to do *Sadhana* (meditation) for the realization of god. For *Sadhana*, a sound body and a sound mind are most essential. Fasts help a great deal in keeping the body in the best state of health. With all the best possible precautions, it is very difficult to avoid committing mistakes in regard to the food that we take. A man with great self-control may be moderate in food; but there are various other causes which he cannot avoid and thus his health gets impaired.

If there is even the least symptom of disease in the body, it is a signal to fast for a day or two. Animals, which depend only upon nature, fast naturally if there is any disease, and cure themselves by natural means, e.g., sunlight and fresh air, fast and rest.

Cold, headache, slight feverishness, a little cough, loaded colon, etc. are some of the signs of diseases, which, if neglected in the beginning, may take a serious form. To avert this impending danger, our *Shastras* have enjoined fasts on Ekadasi, Pradosha, Shivaratri, Poornima,

Amavasya and on other particular days in the week for the propitiation of particular deities. One should observe fast on any one or more of these days. But, as few persons are now in the habit of keeping the Indian almanac, they may observe fasts on any weekday as it suits their work and convenience.

Really, fast is a fast-curing agent for many of the ailments. It gives some rest to the stomach and eliminates toxins from the body. It cleanses the body and thus makes it more energetic. It can cure many diseases. Much care is required in observing long fasts. They should be observed under the guidance of an expert; otherwise if there is any mistake in their observance, there is every possibility of more harm than good being done to the system. Two or three days' fast can be observed without the guidance of an expert.

In this age, when there is a great lack of self-control, a weekly fast on any day, living on fruit juice, is much better and convenient; and this should be necessarily observed. If even this is found difficult, a half-day fast should invariably be observed by all persons. They should take fruit juice in the morning and in the noon, and have their usual meal before sunset; or they should have their usual meal in the morning and take no cooked food in the evening, and take juice of fruits only. By gradual practice, they should learn to fast one day in the week without taking any solid food.

Fast for over a week not only cleanses the body, but gives us more energy and power and also spiritual strength.

The Ekadasi, or Saturday, the Sabbath Day, whichever suits you best, can be observed as a fasting day. Keep it at definite and regular intervals as it suits you. It gives the worldly-minded man more and more happiness just as the sage, who has nothing to ask for. It gives him altogether a different kind of health. It is absurd to imagine that you are growing weak for want of food. Indirectly you grow stronger day by day both physically and mentally through fasting.

Fasting gives clearness of insight into subjects, a mirror for the vision; it bestows in the human machine an activity all anew. You must hear a course of discourses by a man who has practised fast. You somehow develop awe, you have an inexplicable liking for him for no reason and you are proud of having him in your presence all for the divinity that has unconsciously crept into him without his knowledge.

Festivals
Their Importance

Look at nature: there is existence enjoying Holi everyday, and celebrating Diwali everyday. In nature the colours flow afresh everyday; new flowers open each morning. Even before the old leaves fall, the new buds are bursting out and the new shoots are springing up. The festival does not stop even for a moment–it is non-stop, every moment is Diwali.

Such will be the life of a religious person. He will be festive each moment– he is grateful that he is. His every breath is an expression of gratitude and benediction and this is a by-product of witnessing. Witnessing means seeing from a distance whatever is happening. The day you begin to see that you are beyond all that which is surrounding you each moment, you have transcended. You will know that you are flowing with the supreme energy of existence.

India has numerous national, regional, local, religious, seasonal and social festivities. This is not surprising, considering the fact that India is the land of gods, goddesses, saints, *gurus* and prophets. All these festivals are characterized by colour, gaiety, celebrations, feasts and a variety of prayers and rituals. It may not be out of place to describe India as 'a land of festivals'. Since India is a multi-religious and multi-lingual country, it is but natural to find festivals of all major religions in the world being celebrated in India. Thus, we come across Holi, Dussehra, Janmashtami, Hanuman Jayanti, Ganesh Charurthi, Eid-Ul-Fitr, Muharram, Shivaratri, Buddha Jayanti, Jamshed Navroz, Christmas and Diwali, all celebrated in the spirit of harmony and national oneness. There is also a stream of secular or non-religious festivals like the harvest festivals of Baisakhi and Pongal-Sankranti, Raksha Bandhan, Karwa Chauth, etc.

India, the vibrant land of mythological tales of gods and goddesses and a thousand beliefs, has evolved over centuries as a mystic land of festivals. Every occasion you can dream of is celebrated with gaiety. These colourful and happy festivals bind the people of the nation across various states and religions in a unique way and provide a spectacle that cannot be experienced anywhere else in the world.

India is a land of festivity – religious as well as folkloristic. Whether you go to the East or the West, North or the South you would be able to enjoy every month a festival or a fair. Be it cultural or religious, it gives everyone an opportunity to enjoy and join the festivity.

The Hindu festivals, fasts, rituals, holy baths and the observance of sacred days are part and parcel of the great cultural heritage of India. They are a great source of spiritual and moral enrichment. They are deep-rooted in our traditions and ideals that have left deep impact on Indian culture and civilization.

Festivals are a celebration of life itself. In India, festivals are celebrated with gusto, devotion and passion.

Festivals are an intrinsic part of the Indian ethos. They reflect the diversity of celebrations in a multi-cultural nation which values sentiments, respects traditions and fosters community living. Every occasion, from the harvesting of crops to welcoming the seasons or marking the full moon, is a reason to celebrate.

Festivals are characterised by folk music and dances, feasts, prayers and rituals. Indian festivals are celebrated according to the solar and lunar calendars. Consequently, dates can vary in the Gregorian calendar.

Customs and Traditions
A Prologue

Indian culture is admired and respected all over the world for its beauty and profundity. Almost every Indian custom and tradition has either a scientific, logical, historical, social or spiritual significance. Understanding this lends meaning to an otherwise traditional following of the customs which are often misunderstood to be mere superstitions that fade away in time.

A unique feature of Indian culture is its self-rejuvenating capacity. Customs that are obsolete are gradually dropped as seen in the instances of human sacrifice as well as animal sacrifice, to a large extent, *sati*, unsociability etc. This culture tailors itself constantly to take the best of the modern, technological age without losing its roots.

It is this adaptability that has enabled India to be recognized as one of the world's oldest living civilizations. The customs and traditions given are simple, enduring ones, that have lasted the test of time and are an integral part of many an Indian home even today.

Some of the major customs and traditions are explained in the following passages:

NAMASTE

The word '*Namaste*' is formed by joining '*namah*' and '*te*'. The meaning of '*namah*' is to bend and bow one's head, and '*te*' means '*tere liye*', for thou. '*Te*' is singular of *chaturthi* of *yushmat* word, which in Hindi means '*tu*'. In fact, the word in itself is small, incomplete and a symbol of slavery. Now any intelligent man can understand that if an elderly person addresses someone younger to him with '*Namaste*', it is respect in reverse order. The reason is that, in the cultures in the world, the bowing of head by the parents before their children, by the teacher before his disciple and by the husband before his wife is considered indiscreet. In Indian culture if you address an old man as '*tu*', it is as good as killing him, and an inexcusable crime.

The real meeting between people is the meeting of their minds. When we greet, we do so by saying '*namaste*', which means "May our minds meet," indicated by folded palms placed before the chest. The bowing down of head indicates the gracious form of extending friendship in love and humility. The gesture is often accompanied by words like "*Ram-Ram*", "*Jai Sri Krishna*", "*Namoh Narayana*", "*Jai Siya Ram*", "*Om Shanti*" etc. indicating the recognition of divinity.

The spiritual meaning of *Namaste* is that the life force, the divinity, self or the lord is the same in all creatures.

Handshake, as a blind following of the West, is not desirable. This practice has proved very dangerous in transmission of contagious diseases. Now people in the West shake hands with gloves on. According to Indian beliefs, by shaking hands with others you are earthing your accumulated divine strength. So handshake is a wrong and painful practice.

PIPAL WORSHIP

As mentioned in *Shrimad Bhagvad Geeta*, Lord Krishna himself says that among trees *Pipal* is the most sacred tree. Therefore, devout Hindus get ready even to lay down their lives happily in defense of a Pipal tree. The *Pipal* tree is considered as the abode of Lord Vishnu.

According to *Skandapurana*, Vishnu lives in the roots of *Pipal*, Keshav (Krishna) in its trunk, Narayan in the branches, Lord Hari in the leaves, and all the other gods in the fruits of *Pipal*. This tree is the concrete and living form of Shri Vishnu. Persons of great souls serve its pious roots. Its shelter, enriched with virtues and fulfilling all wishes, eliminates thousands of sins of men.

IMPORTANCE OF STRING (*MALA*)

In *Sanatan Dharma* of Hindus the importance of string (*mala*) is not limited to knowing the number of the *mantras*. Our *Maharshis* went beyond and searched, and ordained wearing strings of medicinal stones, herbs and divine trees.

According to *Tantra-saar*, the string or garland of *kamalaksha (kamal-gatta)* (lotus seed) destroys the enemy. A string made of *kusha* knots removes sins. A string of Jiyapeta (Jeevaputra), worn along with amulets of *Santan-gopal* and with recitation of Lord's names bestows a son. A string of rubies gives wealth. A string of *rudraksha*, worn and with recitation of *Mahamrityunjaya mantra*, removes diseases and gives a long life. A string of *haridra* is worn for removing the obstacles and eliminating enemies. For killing others and doing *tamasi* (bad) deeds a string made of snake bones is used. A string of marble is good for learning and attracting others. A string of *tulsi* and tiny conches is prescribed for pleasing Shri Krishna and Vishnu. A string of tiger's nail, gold, silver and copper coins is used for saving children from evil eye and many infectious diseases.

PROSTRATION BEFORE ELDERS, SPECIALLY PARENTS

Touching the feet in prostration is a sign of respect for the age, maturity, nobility and divinity that our elders personify. It shows our recognition of their selfless love for us and the sacrifices that they have done for us. Prostration is done daily, when we meet daily and on important occasions.

When we prostrate with humility and respect, we invoke the good wishes and blessings of elders which flow in the form of positive energy to envelop us.

This tradition thus creates an environment of mutual love and respect among people ensuring harmony in the family and society.

LIGHTING A LAMP

Light is the symbol of knowledge, and darkness that of ignorance. A lamp is lit in homes once or twice daily at dawn and dusk, in front of the gods. In a few homes, it is continuously lit, "*akhanda deep*". All the auspicious occasions are inaugurated with lighting a lamp. Knowledge removes ignorance just as light removes darkness. Hence we light the lamp to bring knowledge as the greatest of all forms of wealth. Therefore, we keep a lamp lit during all auspicious occasions as a witness to our thoughts and actions.

The traditional oil lamp has spiritual significance against lighting an electric bulb or tubelights. It is said the "*ghee*" or oil in lamp signifies our "*vaasnas*" while wick *(batti)* signifies the ego. When a lamp is lit, our *vaasnas* are slowing exhausted and ego perishes.

CHANTING *OM* AND *HARI OM*

There is a *Vedic* tradition to pronounce 'Hari Om' before the chanting of a *mantra* at the beginning of *Veda path* (study of the *Vedas*). Incorrect pronunciation of the Vedas causes a defect, named *Mahapatak*. It is compulsory to pronounce *Hari Om* in the beginning and end in order to remove the possible defect of mis-pronunciation. It is stated in *Shrimad Bhagwat*:

Sarvam karoti nishchhidram nam sankirtanam hareh
With the *sankirtan* (musical recital) of *Hari Om*, all these defects and impediments are removed which may crop up in a religious ceremony due to improper chanting of *mantras*, procedure, arrangement, place, time and things.

Om is the most chanted sacred sound in India. It has a profound effect on the body and mind of the one who chants. All the auspicious actions are started with *Om*. It is repeated as a *mantra*. The sound emerging from the vocal chords starts from the base of the throat as "A". With the coming together of the lips, "U" is formed and when the lips are closed, all sound ends in "M".

The *Om* chant should have the resounding sound of a bell *(aaooomm)*. It fills the mind with peace. Om is written in different ways. It also symbolizes Lord Ganesha.

GANESH WORSHIP FIRST

There is not a single activity in *Sanatan Dharma* which is performed without the worship of Ganapati first. Resultingly, Shri Ganesh became a synonym of beginning.

He is the first to be worshipped among all gods due to his rare intellectual brilliance. Accoring to *Yagyavalkya Smriti*, after the worship of Ganesh, all the nine *grahas* should be properly worshipped. This leads to good results of all activities and attainment of wealth.

JANEU

The word *janeu*, which is a brief form of *yagyopaveeta*, is formed with a combination of *yajna*, synonym for *yagya* (from which ya is dropped) and *upaveeta* (from which *paveeta* has been dropped). In common parlance and in a slightly deformed shape, in rural areas, people call *yagyopaveeta* as *janeu*.

Janeu is a sacred thread worn by Hindu males from the time they reach adolescence and the related ritual is performed by a teacher who makes him take certain vows aimed at concentrating on education etc.

BHASMA (ASH)

Bhasma means our sins are destroyed and the lord is remembered. "*Bhasma*" is the ash from the "*homa*" where sandalwood along with *ghee* and other herbs are offered as wor-

HINDU FASTS & FESTIVALS   16

ship of the lord. Many consume a pinch of *Bhasma* when they receive it.

Bha implies *Bharatsanam* (to destroy) and *Sma* implies *Smaranam* (to remember): Thus meaning destruction of the evil and remembrance of divine. *Bhasma* is also called "*Vibhuti*" (glory).

The ash we apply indicates that we should burn false identification with the body and become free of the limitations of birth and death. This also reminds us that the body is perishable and one day it will reduce to ashes.

Bhasma is specially associated with lord Shiva who applies it all over his body. *Bhasma* has also medicinal value and is used in many Ayurvedic medicines. It absorbs excess moisture from the body and prevents cold and headaches.

WATCHING DHRUV

In Indian culture there is a tradition of having Dhruvdarshan, seeing 'Dhruv' star which has always a fixed and permanent position. It bestows long life to husband when it is watched by a married woman, while its steadfast character helps the couple in performing their marital duties towards each other. This pious message is bestowed on the couple through blessings of seven *rishis*. Just as Dhruv is fixed, likewise the bride's *suhag* (husband) should be fixed and permanent. Dhruv is steadfast and committed, likewise the bride and groom should be steadfast and committed in the performance of their duties and regulations of married life. This pious message is passed on to bride and groom, along with the blessings of seven *rishis*, at the time of their marriage.

OFFER *BHOG* TO GOD

Whatever food and water we are reciving, we should consider it as God's gift and offer it to Him first. This is not only being rightly grateful to Him, but a good human trait also.

A father had two sons, Chunnu and Annu. There was some festivity at home. Both of them insisted and got some pocket money from their father. Both of them went to their village fair. Chunnu bought some *pakoris* (fried eatables) from his pocket money and ate them alone. Annu bought some *rewaris* (sweets). He was reminded of his father's instructions that one should not eat things alone. He ran back home and offered *rewaris* to his father who was sitting with his friends. He said to his father, '*Pitaji*, you please take some of these first'. The father did not touch the *rewaris*, but he was touched by this little gesture. He was happy on seeing the obedience of his son. His friends also appreciated this gesture of his son and gave him money in reward. In the evening Chunnu was admonished for his eating alone, and he was never given extra money again, to spend.

Chunnu and Annu are none other than two sons of God: one an atheist, and the other a theist, and father, the God. Both of them cry and beg for money from their father. Atheist son Chunnu eats alone all the things provided by nature, but the theist son remembers the instructions of the *Vedas* and scriptures, distributes his things to gods, others and after that eats them as *prasad* from God. The Lord, Shriman Narayan, gets pleased and bestows upon such persons more and more *Riddhi-Siddhi* (wealth and success). After offering food to God, accepting it as His *prasad* makes that food divine. The offer of *bhog* to God is the chief characteristic of theism.

CHANTING "*SHANTI*" THRICE

It is generally believed that what is said thrice comes true. In the law courts also, one who takes the witness box says, "I shall speak the truth, the whole truth and nothing but the truth." We chant "*Shanti*" thrice to emphasise our intense desire for peace.

Shanti, meaning peace, is a natural state of being. Peace already exists in a place until someone makes noise and causes agitations. When agitations end, peace is naturally experienced since it was already there. Peace within or without seems very hard to attain because it is covered by our own agitations. To invoke peace, we chant prayers to end our troubles and peace is experienced internally, irrespective of the external disturbances and all such prayers end by chanting "*Shanti*", thrice.

It is said that all our troubles and sorrows originate from three sources: First of all, *Aadhidaivika* – the unseen divine forces over which we have no control like tsunami, earthquakes, floods, volcanic eruptions etc. Secondly, *Aadhibhautika:* known factors like accidents, human contacts, pollution etc. And thirdly, *Aadhyaatmika:* problems of our bodies and minds like diseases, anger, frustration etc.

Shanti is chanted loudly for the first time addressing the unseen forces, second time, a little softer, directing to our immediate surroundings and, third time, we chant *Shanti* in the softest tone, to address ourselves.

CONCH BLOWING

A conch is blown during wars and battles to intimidate and finally destroy the enemy. One who blows the conch at the time of worship has all his sins destroyed, and he enjoys happiness with Lord Vishnu.

When the conch is blown, the primordial sound of *OM* emanates. *Om* is an auspicious sound that was chanted by the Lord before creating the world. It represents the world and the truth behind it.

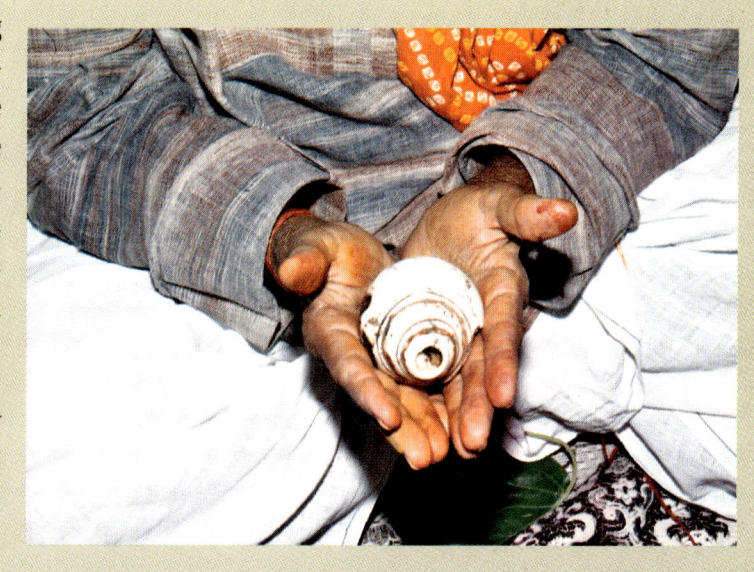

Another well-known purpose of blowing the conch and other instruments, known traditionally to produce auspicious sounds, is to drown or mask any prevailing negativity or noises that may disturb or upset the atmosphere or the minds of worshippers. The conch is placed at the altar in temples and homes, next to the Lord as a symbol of *Naada*

Brahma, the *Vedas, Om, dharma,* victory and auspiciousness. It is often used to offer devotees sanctified water to raise their minds to the highest truth.

All these religious beliefs have a scientific basis. Scientists believe that the rays of the sun are an impediment in the propagation of sound. That's why a conch is blown either in the morning or evening when sun rays are of low intensity. The sound of conch kills all the germs of various diseases, due to its vibration of a particular high frequency.

Indian scientist Jagadis Chandra Bose has proved this fact through experiments. Hearing the sound of conch is panacea for removing dumbness and stammering. A person who regularly blows conch never suffers from breathing problem, asthma or any lung diseases. The sound of conch is highly beneficial in several cases of diseases. Regular conch sound is very useful in purifying air, atmosphere and environment.

TULSI WORSHIP

Most of the religious minded families have a *Tulsi* plant in their *aangan* (courtyard). It gives a Hindu family a special identity. Women by worshipping it bring prosperity in their family. When Shri Hanuman, the devotee of Lord Ram, entered Lanka looking for Sita, he saw a *Tulsi* plant in the courtyard of a house and could make out how pious the householder must be and whose help he sought later.

The worship of *Tulsi* has been going on as a very ancient tradition. Those who do not have their own children arrange *Tulsi* marriage. Lord Vishnu cannot be worshipped without offering *Tulsi* leaves. Leaves of *Tulsi* are a must in *bhog* for Lord Vishnu and in *charanamrit* and *panchamrit*. Without it, *bhog* is not offered to gods. The water of the Ganges and *Tulsi* leaves are given to a person lying on death bed. No other plant has such religious significance as *Tulsi*.

There is a scientific secret behind all these religious beliefs. *Tulsi* is a divine medicinal plant and like *kasturi* (musk) it has the power to infuse life into a dead man. Terminal diseases such as cancer can be cured by *Tulsi*. Great values of *Tulsi* find a mention in books of Ayurveda. Its leaves boiled in water, if taken during fever, cold, cough and malaria, provide immediate relief. *Tulsi* leaves have a remarkable property of preventing infectious diseases. When it is placed in *bhog* (offering to gods), it doesn't rot or go sour. When it is mixed in *panchamrit* or *charanamrit*, it does not turn sour or develop germs for a long period. *Tulsi manjaris* (pods) give out a peculiar scent which repels poisonous snakes. It is worshipped for its medicinal properties.

According to a book titled *Ranvir Bhakti Ratnakar*: "Wherever the wind scented by *Tulsi* blows, it purifies all directions, and makes all the four forms of life – *udhbij, swedaj, andaj* and *jara* – full of zest and spirit." According to another book, *Kriyayogasar,* the very touch of *Tulsi* kills the germs of malaria and many other diseases immediately.

OFFERING COCONUT AT RELIGIOUS CEREMONIES

Long back, animals were sacrificed, symbolizing the offering of our animalistic tendencies to our lord but, with the passage of time, this practice got faded away and we started offering coconut instead, after removing the fibre covering of the dried coconut, as a token of that earlier practice.

Coconut is offered on occasions like weddings, festivals, on purchasing new vehicles, starting the construction of buildings, bridges or big projects etc. Coconut is placed on a water-filled "*kalash*" (pot) on such occasions for worshipping.

The marks on the coconut make it look like the head of a human being and when it is broken, it symbolizes breaking of our ego. The water within, representing the inner tendencies, is offered along with the white kernel–the mind, to the Lord. A mind thus purified by the touch of the Lord is used as *prasad*.

Coconut also symbolizes selfless servcice as every part of its tree-trunk, leaves, fruits, coir etc. is used in many ways like making house thatches, mats, dishes, oil, soap etc. The marks on the coconut are even thought to represent the three-eyed Lord Shiva and, therefore, it is considered to be a means to fulfil our desires.

CUSTOMS AND TRADITIONS - A PROLOGUE

RINGING BELL IN TEMPLES AND HOMES

The ringing of the bell produces what is regarded as an auspicious sound. It produces the sound of *Om*, the universal name of the Lord. There should be auspiciousness within and without, to gain the vision of the Lord who is all-auspiciousness.

In all temples, there are bells hung at the entrance gate and the devotees ring the bell as soon as they enter for the *darshan* of Lord.

The bells are not for awakening the Lord as He never sleeps. Nor there is any need to take permission from the God by ringing bells. It is meant only to arouse the prevailing auspiciousness. Even while doing the ritualistic *aarati*, we ring the bell. It is sometimes accompanied by the auspicious sounds of the conch and other musical instruments.

PRADAKSHINA

When we visit a temple, after offering prayers, we circumambulate the sanctum sanctorum and this is called *pradakshina* One can not make a circle without the centre point. Recognising Him as the central point in our lives, we go about doing our daily chores. This is the significance of *pradakshina*.

As we do *pradakshina* in a clockwise direction, the Lord is always on our right. In India, the right side symbolises auspiciousness. It is a telling fact that even in the English language it is called the right side and not the wrong one. So, as we circumambulate the sanctum sanctorum, we remind ourselves to lead an auspicious life of righteousness, with the Lord who is the indispensable source of help and strength, as our guide – the right hand the *dharma* aspect of our lives.

A PRAYER ROOM IN HOMES

Brahma is the owner of the entire "*Brahmand*" including planet Earth. He is therefore the true owner of the house we live in and the prayer room is the master room of the house. We are mere occupants of His property. This notion rids us of false pride and possessiveness.

Most Indian homes have a prayer room and a lamp is lit to worship the Lord every morning and evening. Special worship is done on auspicious occasions like birthdays, anniversaries, festivals and the like. Every member of the family–young or old–communicates with and worships the Supreme Being in prayer room.

As we need bedroom, drawing room etc. and decorate these to our taste, so too for the purpose of meditation, worship and prayer, we should have a conducive atmosphere – hence the need for a prayer room. The ideal attitude to have is to regard the Lord as the true owner of our homes and us as caretakers of His home. Also the Lord is all-pervading. To remind us that He resides in our homes with us, we have prayer rooms. Without the grace of the Lord, no task can be successfully or easily accomplished. We invoke His grace by communicating with Him in the prayer room each day and on special occasions.

Sacred thoughts and sound vibrations pervade the place and influence the minds of those who spend time there. Spiritual thoughts and vibrations accumulated through regular meditation, worship and chanting done there pervade the prayer room.

WORSHIPPING SNAKES

According to ancient Hindu beliefs, the whole earth rests on the hood of Sheshnag, the legendry snake. So a snake of silver is made and the spirit of Sheshnag is infused in it and it is placed in the foundation of new constructions. The thought behind it is that just as Sheshnag is holding the earth steadfast, so should the foundation of the building be steadfast on the hood of this snake. *Patal-lok* is below the earth. The master of the *Patal-lok* is snake. Therefore, snake is worshipped for elimination of evil effects. Since Sheshnag lives in *Ksheer-sagar*, ocean of milk, therefore, by putting milk, curd and ghee in the *kalash* as representation of *ksheer-sagar* and charming it with *mantras*, gods are invoked. Therefore in this *Vishnu-kalash*, a coin with the image of Lakshmi is put and the *Kalash* is placed inside the ground. The entire ritual of foundation worship is based on these beliefs.

WHY WE WORSHIP IDOL?

Idol worship is a means of withdrawing mind from all sides and concentrating on God. The quietness of mind is known as *dhyana*. *Samadhi* implies getting settled in *Brahma*. Idol is required if mind does not quieten and settle without it. There is no alternative to idol worship to control the mind, and help it acquire knowledge and consciousness to settle.

Not only this, psychologists say that the idol is required for right feeling to come into play. Imagine a man has photos of three women in his hands. One is of his mother, the second one is that of his wife and the third one is that of his sister. The feeling in that man's mind will vary according to the picture he sees. His mother's photograph will stir up his respect and affection, while his sister's photograph will trigger his sense of duty and love towards his sister. On the other hand, his wife's photograph will arouse his romantic feelings.

Eklavya built the statue of Dronacharya and worshipped him as his teacher, and became a greater expert in archery than Arjuna. On instructions from Narad, Dhruva made a statue and worshipped it and saw God in reality through this medium.

Not only in *Sanatan Dharma*, idol worship is also prevalent in other religions of the world. Christians worship the Holy Cross. Our Muslim brethren kiss *Sangey Asvad* in Mecca Sharif. They offer floral garlands on graves *(dargah)*. Sikhs worship *Guru Granth Sahib*.

Basant Panchami

Basant Panchami heralds the advent of spring and is dedicated to Goddess Saraswati. This festival marks the first day of spring. *Vasant* means the spring. The fields are mustard yellow with the ripening of crops. Yellow is an auspicious colour – a colour of spirituality. Basant Panchami falls on the fifth day of the bright half of *Magh* (Jan-Feb). Saraswati is the consort of Lord Brahma and is the goddess of wisdom and knowledge. She is the personification of knowledge – arts, science and crafts. She represents *Shakti*, creativity and inspiration and presents herself when the weather is complacent and nature is in its full grandeur. It is a season of inspiration and passion.

CELEBRATIONS

The most significant aspect of this day is that Hindu children are taught reading and writing their first words on this day – as it is considered an auspicious day to begin a child's education. Educational institutions organize special prayers for Saraswati on this day.

Saintly people and people inclined towards spiritual progress attach great importance to the worship of Goddess Saraswati. As a practice, educated people and men of principle worship Goddess Saraswati for spiritual enlightenment. In their opinion, there can be no comparison between the king and the learned or the spiritually advanced. They believe that the king is honoured within his kingdom, whereas the learned are respected or worshipped throughout the world.

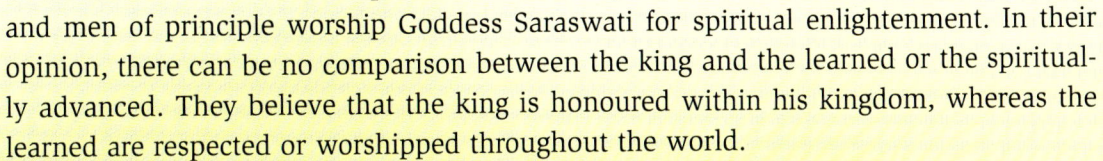

RITUALS

There are various rituals that are followed in the worshipping of Goddess Saraswati. The one common ritual followed by all the worshippers is that the idol of the goddess is clothed in white, the other predominant colour in the celebrations being yellow, to indicate the onset of spring and the blossoming of mustard flowers. Flowers and wild berries are offered to the goddess and students place their books before the deity and do not do any reading or writing that day. An elaborate *puja*, with sandalwood, *ghee*, joss sticks, and incense is done to the sound of *shlokas*, conch shells, and drums. A ritual not connected to the worship but equally essential to the celebration is that of flying kites on this day.

The offerings to the goddess are mainly fruits – most significant being berries from the wild plum tree. Sweets must include puffed rice, jaggery and yogurt.

The priest using special wood, ghee, joss sticks and incense does a havan. Absence of any burnt smell signifies the success of the *puja*. A *diya* or lamp is also kept lit along with the *bhog*.

A handful of flowers particularly marigold and flame of the forest is given to each devotee to offer to the goddess as "*pushpanjali*". The offering is done in batches of devotees who repeat *mantras* after the priest.

The lit lamp used during the *Arati* is passed around for each devotee and touching the heads.

Nobody touches books on that day. This signifies that the goddess is blessing the books placed in front of her that day.

Holi Festival

Amongst India's innumerable festivals, Holi ranks as the most colourful. It celebrates the arrival of spring and death of demoness Holika; it is a celebration of joy and hope. Holi provides a refreshing respite from the mundane norms as people from all walks of life enjoy themselves. In a tightknit community, it also provides a good opportunity for giving a go-by to any earlier unpleasantness, by way of applying colours on each other and embracing.

Holi continues to be celebrated with great vigour throughout India. Countless Hindi films have brought the vibrant colours of the festival to the screen. Indians all over the world eagerly await the festival of colours, as bonfires are lit to banish the cold dark nights of winter and usher in warmer spring. Dulhendi, day after Holi, is the actual festival of colours, when everything in sight is covered in a riot of colours.

HISTORY

According to legend, Hiranyakashipu was a very powerful demon. In his fight against the gods, he had defeated them and, because of this, he became very egoistic and had issued an order that no one should pray to gods or even take the name of gods, particularly God Vishnu. Due to fear people started praying him. His son Prahlad was a true devotee of God. He didn't obey his father's order. Hiranyakashipu got angry on him and ordered for the most rigorous punishments to him. But this did no harm to Prahlad. Hiranyakashipu had a sister by the name of Holika. She had been granted a boon that fire will do no harm to her, being a noble soul. Hiranyakashipu ordered Holika to take Prahlad on her lap and sit on a bed of fire. Surprisingly, Holika was burnt in the fire and Prahlad survived, with no harm done to him. As a remembrance to that event, people celebrate Holi by burning wood and pray to Goddess Holi for their well-being.

The festival of Holi begins on Dwadashi – the twelfth day of the waxing moon in the month of Phalgun. Spirits run high as the preparations for the festivities begin. As a custom, mothers make new clothes for their married daughters. Coloured powder *(Gulal)* is bought and prepared, long syringes called '*pichkaris*' are made ready and water balloons are bought and filled. Preparations are made to cook special food items that are exclusively meant for this festival.

Twin towns of Nandagaon (where Lord Krishna grew up) and Barsana (where Radha grew up), near Mathura, are the epicentre of the celebrations. Lord Krishna, while growing up in Nandgaon, popularized the festival with his ingenious pranks. *Gopies* responded with equal enthusiasm and the festivities have continued ever since. Role reversal, feminism etc. are accepted customs for the duration of the festival. Men and women clash in a colourful display of battle of the sexes. Celebrations start here a week earlier than in rest of India. Men of Nandagaon raid Barsana with hopes of raising their flag over Radhika temple. They receive a thunderous welcome as the women of Barsana greet them with long wooden sticks. The men are soundly beaten as they attempt to rush through the town to reach the relative safety of Radhikaji's temple. Men are well padded, as they are not allowed to retaliate.

In this mock battle, men try their best not to be captured. Unlucky captives can be forcibly led away, thrashed and dressed in female attire before being made to dance.

The festival moves on to other parts of *Vraj*. Soon enough, it is *Dulhendi* and entire India celebrates the joys of spring as the "festival of colour".

HOLI FESTIVAL

The colourful festival is celebrated in most parts of India during February-March (in the month of Phalgun, according to the Hindu calendar). The celebrations vary, depending on the region and local traditions but the common element is exchange of colours.

CELEBRATIONS

It is observed on the full moon night of Phalgun. It marks the end of winter and the advent of spring season. It is a two-day festival. On the first night, a bonefire is lighted in the evening or at night, and people circumambulate it which is known as *pradakshina*. Children make merry, womenfolk and men sing in gay abandon to the accompaniment of cymbals and drums. In this fun-filled atmosphere, people play practical jokes on one another.

The next day, people amuse themselves by splashing coloured water and throwing coloured powder on their friends, relatives, neighbours and even passers-by. Noisy and colourful processions are taken out through the streets. Amongst the elite it is characterized by songs, music, floral decoration and splashing of perfumed water. Sweets and visits are exchanged and cold drinks prepared at home are served liberally. People forget all enmity and embrace each other, with warmth and love, and renew their friendship. On this day, people bake and eat new corn for the first time in the season.

In Bengal, Holi is celebrated as Dol Purnima. This festival is dedicated to Sri Krishna. On this auspicious day, an image of Krishna, richly adorned and besmeared with

HINDU FASTS & FESTIVALS 30

coloured powder, is taken out in procession, in a swinging palanquin, decorated with flowers, leaves, coloured clothes and paper. The procession proceeds forward to the accompaniment of music, blaring of conch shells, trumpets and shouts of '*Jai*' (victory).

Dol Purnima becomes all the more significant for Bengalis, because this is also the birthday of Chaitanya Mahaprabhu (1485-1533AD). He was a great Vaishnava saint, who popularized modern *sankirtana*. He elevated the passion of Radha and Krishna to a high spiritual plane. He underlined emotion at the cost of the ceremonial side of devotion. Followers of Chaitanya School of Vaishnavism believe Chaitanya to be the manifestation of Krishna. Chaitanya Mahaprabhu believed that the essence of *sadhana* is always the loving remembrance of Hari.

Lohri Festival

The history of Lohri, a seasonal festival of North India, is as old as that of the Indus Valley civilization itself. The festival of Lohri marks the beginning of the end of the winter and the coming of spring and the new year. The fires lit at night, the hand warming, the song and dance and the coming together of an otherwise atomized community, are only some of the features of this festival. The Lohri of North India coincides with Pongal in Tamil Nadu, Makar Sankranti in Bengal, Magha Bihu in Assam, Tai Pongal in Kerala, all are celebrated on the same auspicious day.

There are some interesting socio-cultural folk legends connected with Lohri. According to the cultural history of Punjab, Bhatti, a Rajput tribe, during the reign of Akbar, inhabited north-eastern regions. Dulla Bhatti, Raja of one region called Pindi Bhattian, was put to death by the Mughal king for revolting against him. The tribal *mirasis* (street singers) trace the history of the tribe and interestingly claim Maharaja Ranjit Singh as one of its scions.

Dulla Bhatti, like Robinhood, robbed the rich and gave to the poor. The people of the area loved and respected him. He once rescued a girl from kidnappers and adopted her as his daughter. His people would remember their hero every year on Lohri. Groups of children moved from door to door, singing the Dulla Bhatti folk-song: "*Dulla Bhatti ho! Dulle ne dhi viyahi ho! Ser shakar pai ho!*" (Dulla gave his daughter a kilo of sugar as a marriage gift).

Some believe that Lohri has derived its name from Loi, the wife of Sant Kabir, for in rural Punjab, Lohri is pronounced as *Lohi*. Others believe that *Lohri* comes from the word *loh*, a thick iron sheet tawa used for baking *chapattis* for community feasts. Another legend says that Holika and Lohri were sisters. While the former perished in the Holi fire, the latter survived. Eating of *til* (sesame seeds) and *rorhi* (jaggery) is considered to be essential on this day. Perhaps the words *til* and *rorhi* merged to become *tilorhi*, which eventually got shortened to *Lohri*

Lohri is essentially a festival dedicated to the gods of fire and the sun god. It is the time when the sun transits the zodiac sign *Makar* (Capricorn), and moves towards the north. In astrological terms, this is referred to as the sun becoming Uttarayan. The new configuration lessens the ferocity of winter, and brings warmth to earth. It is to ward off the bitter chill of the month of January that people light bonfires, dance around it in a mood of bonhomie and celebrate Lohri.

Fire is associated with concepts of life and health. Fire, like water, is a symbol of transformation and regeneration. It is the representative of the sun, and is thus related, on the one hand, with rays of light, and on the other with gold. It is capable of stimulating the growth of cornfields and the wellbeing of men and animals. It is the imitative magic purporting to assure the supply of light and heat. It is also an image of energy and spiritual strength. That is why the Lohri fire gets sanctified and is venerated like a deity. On this occasion, people offer peanuts, popcorn and sweets made of *til, chirva, gajak* and *revri* – to propitiate the fire god.

Lohri has great social significance. On Makar Sankranti, a day after, the new year begins. This time is considered auspicious for marriages and to undertake new ventures. The farmer, comparatively free from his yeoman's duties, takes to fun and frolic. The golden colour of the ripening corn in the fields pleases him.

For the newly-weds and newborn, Lohri is a special occasion. Families of the bride and the groom get-together and celebrate by dancing around the fire and expressing their joy. Lohri is a grand event of social and cultural integration, bringing about unity, amity,

Makar Sakranti

Makar Sankranti is one of the most auspicious days for the Hindus, and is celebrated in almost all parts of the country in myriad cultural forms, with great devotion, fervous & gaiety. Lakhs of people take a dip in holy places like Ganga Sagar and Prayag and pray to Lord Sun. It is celebrated with pomp in southern parts of the country as Pongal, and in Punjab it is celebrated as Lohri & Maghi. People of Gujarat not only look reverentially up to the sun, but also offer thousands of their colourful oblations represented in the form of beautiful kites all over the skyline. They may be trying to reach up to their glorious God or bringing about greater proximity with the one who represents the best. It is a day for which Bhishma Pitamah kept waiting to leave his mortal self.

Makar Sankranti is the day when the glorious Sun God of Hindus begins ascendancy and entry into the northern hemisphere. Sun for the Hindus stands for *Pratyaksha Brahman* – the manifestation of God, who symbolizes the one, non-dual, self-effulgent, glorious divinity blessing one and all, tirelessly. Sun is the one who transcends time and also the one who rotates the proverbial wheel of time. The famous *Gayatri Mantra*, which is chanted everyday by faithful Hindus, is directed to Sun God to bless them with intelligence and wisdom. Sun not only represents God but also stands for an embodiment of knowledge and wisdom. Lord Krishna reveals in *Gita* that this manifested divinity was his first disciple, and we all know it to be indeed a worthy one too. No Sundays for the Sun, may be because one who revels in its very 'being', the very essence of his own Self, is always in the Sunday mood.

ASTROLOGICAL SIGNIFICANCE

Makar means Capricorn and *Sankranti* is transition. There is a *sankranti* every month when the sun passes from one sign of the zodiac to the next. There are twelve signs of the zodiac, and thus there are twelve *sankrantis* as well. Each of these *sankrantis* has its own relative importance but two of these are more important – the *Mesh* (Aries) Sankranti and, the most important, the *Makar* (Capricorn) *Sankranti*. Transition of the Sun from Sagittarius to Capricorn, during the winter solstice in the northern hemisphere is known as *Makar Sankranti*.

From this day begins the six-monthlong *Uttarayana*, considered very auspicious for attaining higher worlds hereafter. While the traditional Indian calendar is primarily based on lunar positions, *Sankranti* is a solar event; so while dates of all festivals keep changing, the Gregorian calendar date of Makar Sankranti is always same, 14th January. Makar Sankranti is celebrated in the Hindu calendar month of Magha. There is another significance of this day – after this day the days start becoming longer and warmer, and thus the chill of winter is on the decline.

RELIGIOUS SIGNIFICANCE

The *Puranas* say that on this day Sun visits the house of his son Shani, who is the *swami* of Makar Rashi. This father-and-son duo does not ordinarily get along nicely, but in spite of the difference between each other Lord Sun makes it a point to meet the son on this day. The father in fact himself comes to his son's house, for a month. This day symbolizes importance of the special relationship of father and son. It is the son who has the responsibility to carry forward his father's dream and the continuity of the family.

From *Uttarayana* starts the 'day' of *Devatas*, while *Dakshinayana* is said to be the 'night' of *Devatas*, so most of the auspicious things are done during this time. *Uttarayana* is also called as *Devayana*, and the next half is called *Pitrayana*.

It was on this day when Lord Vishnu ended the ever increasing terrorism of the *asuras* by finishing them off and burying their heads under the Mandar Parvat. So this occasion also represents the end of negativities and beginning of an era of righteous living.

The great saviour of his ancestors, Maharaj Bhagirath, did great *Tapasya* to bring the holy river Gangaji down on the earth for the redemption of 60,000 sons of Maharaj Sagar, who were burnt to ashes at the Kapil Muni Ashram, near the present day Ganga Sagar. It was on this day that Bhagirath finally did *tarpan* with the Ganges water for his accursed ancestors and thereby liberated them from the curse. After visiting the *Patala* for the redemption of the curse of Bhagirath's ancestors Gangaji finally merged in the Sagar. Even today a very big *Ganga Sagar Mela* is organized every year on this day at the confluence of River Ganga and the Bay of Bengal. Lakhs take dip in the water and do *tarpan* for their ancestors.

Another well-known reference of this day comes from the episode of the great grand-sire of *Mahabharata* fame, Bhishma, when he declared his intent to leave his mortal self on this day. He had the boon of *Ichha-Mrityu* from his father, so he kept lying on the bed of arrows till this day and then left his mortal self on Makar Sankranti day. It is believed that a person, who dies during the period of *Uttarayana*, becomes free from transmigration. So this day is seen as a sure-shot good luck day to start a journey or endeavours for other activities.

HOW TO CELEBRATE

Get up early in the morning, have bath and be ready with water and flowers before sunrise. Worship the rising sun, by offering water and flowers with both the hands and then pray with folded hands by chanting the *Gayatri Mantra* and pray for knowledge, wisdom and enlightenment to rise in similar way as the sun, to greater and greater heights. Pray for blessings to live a dynamic, inspired & righteous life.

Do *tarpan* for your ancestors. See your ancestors in the mind's eyes and offer water to them while praying for their blessings. Resolve to redeem the pledges and pride of your forefathers. Live life in such a way that wherever your forefathers may be, their head is held high by the life and deeds of their children.

Have a special session of meditation, wherein you bring about the awareness of the self-effulgent subjective divinity. Affirm the greatest importance of your spiritual goal very clearly, and pray to God to bless you with the capacity to constantly revel in your true self. May the graph of your life rise like the Uttarayana Sun. May there be greater 'Love and Light' in your life and the world.

Prepare *laddus* or other sweets of *til* and *gur* and offer them to your friends & relatives. See to it that your 'well-being prayer for all' gets manifested in action and deeds.

Have the lunch of *Khichiri*. This stands for inculcating simplicity in your life and habits.

Give some *daan* on this day to someone who truly deserves.

If you have a married son, visit him at his place and give presents to the son and the daughter-in-law. If it is not possible to visit, then organize to send presents to them to express your love and affection for them. Work to properly cultivate the generation, which has to carry forward all that you cherish and value.

Mahashivratri

The festival of Mahashivratri (literally means the 'Grand Night dedicated for the worship of Lord Shiva') is looked upon with greatest reverence & respect by the devotees of Lord Shiva. This festival is celebrated every year on the 13/14th day in the Krishna Paksha (waning moon fortnight, just before the new moon) of the month of Phalgun. As per the English calendar this is somewhere around February or March.

This day and more so the night is dedicated by the devotees of Lord Shiva for his worship, practice of various austerities & meditation. All the Shiva temples are fully decorated and there are hordes of devotees queuing up to get *darshan* of the Lord and offer their obeisance at his feet, on this special day.

SIGNIFICANCE OF MAHASHIVRATRI

There are several stories which are associated with this special grand night of Lord Shiva:

1. *Samudra Manthan* Story

During *Samudra Manthan* by the gods and demons, a highly toxic poison came out of the ocean. As per the advice of Lord Vishnu, gods approached Lord Shiva and prayed him to protect life by consuming that poison. Pleased with their prayers, out of compassion for living beings, Lord Shiva drank that poison and held it in his throat by binding a knot with a snake. The throat became blue due to the poison (thus Lord Shiva is also known as *Neelakantha*) and Shiva remained unharmed. The wise men advised gods to keep Lord Shiva awake during the night. To keep him awake, the gods took turns, performing various dances and playing music. A vigil was thus kept by the gods in contemplation of Shiva. As the day broke out, Shiva, pleased with their devotion blessed them all, and also said that whosoever worshipped & contemplated on him on this day shall be blessed with the fulfilment of his or her wishes. Since then, on this day and night, devotees observe fast, keep vigil, sing glories of Lord and meditate.

2. Manifested as *Jyotirlinga* on this day:

On this day, manifested the great & also the first ever-effulgent (*Jyotirmaya*) form (*Anala-skanda* or a pillar of fire) of Lord Shiva in front of Lord Vishnu & Brahmaji.

The story goes that once ego infected both Vishnuji and Brahmaji. The result was a clash between both these gods. In order to show their respective superiority they decided to fight it out. Lord Shiva decided to intervene so as to make them realise that there is something more to life than the powers of an embodied being. He manifested in the form of a huge pillar of fire (*Anala-skanda*) whose beginning and end could not be seen. Vishnuji & Brahmaji decided to check what this strange thing was and agreed that whoever returned first, will be considered as supreme. While Vishnuji, in the form of *varaha* (boar), went down towards *patal-loka* to see the end of this pillar, Brahmaji sitting on his swan went up.

Even after years of travel they could not see the beginning or end of this manifestation. Brahmaji saw a leaf falling off, and thought it fell down from the top of the pillar of fire, and returned satisfied that he had seen the starting point. They came back. While Lord Vishnu accepted that he could not see the end, Brahmaji said that he had seen it, which was a lie. Lord Shiva cursed Brahmaji that no one will ever worship him. This manifestation of Lord Shiva in the form of the first effulgent *linga* was on this special day of Mahashivratri, and thus all devotees pray to the effulgent *linga (jyotirlinga)* of Lord Shiva.

3. Reunion of Shiva and Parvati

King Daksha was opposed to his daughter Sati's marriage with Shiva. At a *yagna* (holy sacrifice) the king ignored Shiva and thereby insulted the latter publicly. Sati was so angered by this that she jumped into the sacrificial fire and ended her life. Lord Shiva unleashed his fury at the death of his wife by performing the violent dance, *Tandava*. He wiped out Daksha's kingdom, undertook rigorous penance and retired to the Himalayas. The gods, who feared that the severity of Shiva's penance might bring an end to the world, revived Sati in the new *avatar* of Parvati. Shiva and Parvati married and this reunion is celebrated on Maha Shivaratri.

4. Story of Chitrabhanu

In the *Shanti Parva* of the *Mahabharata*, Bhishma, whilst resting on the bed of arrows and discoursing on *Dharma*, refers to the observance of Maha Shivaratri by King Chitrabhanu. The story goes as follows.

Once upon a time, King Chitrabhanu of the Ikshvaku dynasty, who ruled over the whole of Jambudvipa, was observing a fast with his wife, it being the day of Mahashivratri. The sage Ashtavakra came on a visit to the court of the king.

The sage asked, "O king! Why are you observing a fast today?"

King Chitrabhanu who had the gift of remembering the incidents of his previous birth said to the sage: "In my past birth I was a hunter in Varanasi. My name was Suswara. My livelihood was to kill and sell birds and animals. One day I was roaming the forests in search of animals. I was overtaken by the darkness of night. Unable to return home, I climbed a tree for shelter. It happened to be a *bel* tree. I had shot a deer that day but I had no time to take it home. I bundled it up and tied it to a branch on the tree. As I was tormented by hunger and thirst, I kept awake throughout the night. I shed profuse tears when I thought of my poor wife and children who were starving and anxiously awaiting my return. To pass away the time that night I engaged myself in plucking the *bel* leaves and dropping them down onto the ground.

"The day dawned. I returned home and sold the deer. I bought some food for myself and for my family. I was about to break my fast when a stranger came to me, begging for food. I served him first and then took my food.

"Later, at the time of my death, I saw two messengers of Lord Shiva. They were sent down to conduct my soul to the abode of Lord Shiva. I learnt then, for the first time, of the great merit I had earned by the unconscious worship of Lord Shiva during the night of Shivaratri. They told me that there was a *lingam* under the tree. The leaves I dropped fell on the *lingam*. My tears, which I had shed out of pure sorrow for my family, fell onto the *lingam* and washed it. And I had fasted all day and all night. Thus did I unconsciously worship the Lord. Lord Shiva's messengers took me to the Lord's abode and I lived in the abode of the Lord and enjoyed divine bliss for long ages. I am now reborn as Chitrabhanu."

5. Story of Lubdhak

Another legend is about a tribal named Lubdhak, who was a devotee of Shiva. It was his usual practice to go into the forest to collect firewood. One day he wandered into the forest deeper than usual and night fell before he could come out. It was the night before the no-moon night and the thin crescent moon offered no light. He was not able to find his way in the dark and soon got lost. A hungry tiger smelt him out and with a loud roar made his intentions clear. Lubdhak knew he could not outrun the tiger and so he climbed up a *bel* tree.

In order to keep awake so that he would not fall down in his sleep, he began to pluck the leaves from the *bel* tree and drop them one by one, each time chanting "*Om Namah Shivaya*", which means I bow down to Shiva. In this manner, he passed the night. Until dawn, he had dropped a thousand *bel* leaves. When he descended the tree in the morning, he saw a *lingam*, which he had missed in the dark. Unknowingly he had been dropping leaves on the *lingam*. This was the 14th night of the waxing moon in the month of Phalgun and it came to be celebrated as Mahashivratri.

HOW TO CELEBRATE ?

The devotees of Lord Shiva should preferably do the following things on this day:

1. Observe fast on this day, taking only fruits and milk.
2. Perform elaborate *puja* of Lord Shiva, and perform *Rudrabhisheka*. Chant various hymns and *bhajans* of Lord Shiva.
3. Chant the mantra '*Om Namah Shivaya*' as many times as you can.
4. Practise *Dhyana* for longer periods than the usual routine.
5. Remain more introvert on this day, contemplating about the truths of life.
6. Go for *darshan* of Lord Shiva where he is properly and regularly worshipped.
7. Try to get *darshan* and *satsang* of some learned *Mahatmas*. Offer *sewa* at *Ashrams* and temples.

Pongal

Pongal is a three-day solemn festival, celebrated in South India on Sankranti. Pongal or Makar-Sankranti marks the beginning of the sun's northern course. Then, sun passes into Capricorn from Sagittarius. It is an occasion of great rejoicing and merry-making.

CELEBRATIONS

Pongal festival lasts for three days. The first day is Bhogi-Pongal, the Pongal of joy. On this day people visit each other and exchange sweets, presents, and take an active part in all kinds of amusements.

The second day is Surya-Pongal, or the Pongal of the Sun. This day is dedicated to the Sun. People get up early in the morning to clean their home and take bath. The

HINDU FASTS & FESTIVALS 44

married women then boil rice and milk together and when it begins to simmer, they all shout together, *'Pongal! Pongal!'*. The sweet thus prepared is then offered to Sun and Ganesh. A portion of it is also given to the cows, and then people take it amongst themselves. Once again people exchange visits. On meeting each other they ask, "Has it boiled?" To which they invariably answer "Yes, it is boiled". That is why this festival is called *Pongal,* which means 'to boil.'

The third day is Mattu Pongal or the Pongal of the cows. On this day cows and oxen are worshipped and circumambulated. Their horns are painted in various colours, and garlands of leaves and flowers are hung round their necks. On this day the cows are allowed to graze anywhere they like, without any restraint.

SIGNIFICANCE

Pongal also marks the change of season, and is primarily a harvest festival. India is an agricultural country and cows and oxen play a vital role in agriculture. That is why cows and oxen are worshipped and venerated so much. Pongal also symbolizes the sharing of things with others. The new reaped harvest is shared not only with friends and relatives but also with beasts and birds. They all partake of the cooked food and sweets.

PONGAL 45

Vaikuntha Ekadashi

Vaikuntha Ekadashi is celebrated in the South, in the month of Margashirsha, on both the eleventh day of the bright and as well as the dark fortnight, with great solemnity. Devotees observe fast and remain awake the whole night and do *kirtan*, *jap* and have meditative sessions. In the temple, a gateway is thrown open on this day and the faithful pass through it, and this signifies the entrance into heaven or *Vaikuntha*. Like any other Ekadashi, rice eating is prohibited on this day, because a demon is said to dwell in rice grains on this day. A demon was born out of the sweat that fell down from Brahma's head, and he asked for a place to live in. Brahma told him to go and live in rice grains eaten by people on Ekadsahi and to become a worm in their stomach.

Another legend has it that once a great demon, called Mura, who had 7,000 sons, harassed the gods. The gods prayed to Vishnu for protection against Mura. Vishnu sent Yog Maya to kill the demon and his sons, and she did it successfully. Thereupon, Vishnu said that from then onwards she would be known by the name of *Ekadashi*, and the people who observe fast and piety on this day would be freed from all sins and get a place in heaven.

There is another interesting story about the significance of Vaikuntha Ekadashi. Ambrish, the king of Ayodhya, was a great devotee of Vishnu and always observed Ekadashi vow. Once during Vaikuntha Ekadashi he fasted for three days and was about to break his fast, when Rishi Durvasa appeared at his gate. The king received the *Rishi* with due regards and requested him to have meals. Durvasa readily agreed and went to perform ablution.

The king waited and waited but the *Rishi* did not return and the auspicious moment of breaking the fast was approaching. King Ambrish was in a dilemma. If he did not break his fast before the day ended, his vow would not bear any results, but if he ate anything before the sage arrived, that would be considered as an act of disrespect and disregard to the sage. At last he decided to take a sip of water and break his fast so that it won't be a matter of offence to the sage.

When Durvasa returned, aware of what had happened, he grew angry. In his anger he tore a strand of hair from his head and charged it on the king to destroy him. At once, the discus of Vishnu appeared which destroyed the power of the strand of hair and started chasing the *Rishi* to kill him. Durvasa ran to Brahma and Shiva to seek protection but it proved to be of no avail. Then, he sought refuge with Vishnu himself, but Vishnu said that he was dependent on his devotees and ordered him to go and beg pardon from Ambrish. He did accordingly and was finally saved from doom.

Akshya Tritiya

The fast and festival of Akshya Tritiya (better known as *Akha Teej*) is observed on the third day of the bright half of Vaishakh. '*Akshya*' literally means non-decaying or exempt from decay. The piety and devotion done on this day never decay and secure permanency. This day is also believed to be the first day of the *Satyug*.

It is well known that Indians believe passionately in the theory of *muhurts* or auspicious times to perform sacraments, to make major purchases or to begin new ventures.

In spite of modern technology and changing lifestyles, this dedication to auspicious time remains a prominent feature of Indian life. Akshaya Tritiya, the third day of the bright half of Baishakh, is considered one of the most sacred days of the year.

The word *Akshya* means 'that which never diminishes', hence beginnings made or valuables bought on this day are considered certain to bring luck and success. All over India people celebrate weddings, plan new business ventures, long journeys and other events for this day. Like Diwali, Dussehra and Gudi Padva, Akshya Tritiya is reserved for buying gold, silver and other assets. On this day jewellers keep their shops open well into twilight time to entertain their buyers.

Akshya Tritiya or *Akha Teej* is traditionally the birthday of Parshurama, the sixth incarnation of Vishnu. The *Puranas* tell how he reclaimed land from the sea along the west coast of India by his valour. Even today Goa and the Konkan are called *Parshurama Kshetra*. He then settled 96 selected families there, called Shahanavkuli Brahmins, who are said to have created the cultural heritage of this part of India. In India, gold is regarded as the ultimate symbol of wealth and prosperity. Buying gold and jewellery is a popular activity on Akshya Tritiya, one of the most auspicious days of the year.

HISTORY

Akshya Tritiya day is a very auspicious day. There is no inauspiciousness to be found on this day. Even checking *muhurats* is considered unnecessary, so auspicious is this day. Whatever one does for devotees and for Krishna, that person will get more benefit and its eternal benefit is never lost.

There is one story of a Brahmin: There was a Brahmin who had a very good and beautiful wife. He was poor. With great difficulties they were managing their two times' meals. Also, he did not have children. So, under the strong request of his wife, he went to Vasishtha Muni to know the reason for his suffering. Vasishtha Muni told him that in his previous life, he was very rich and also had many children. But he was very stingy, he was not even spending for his own children. This is the reason for his present condition. Then that Brahmin asked Vasishtha Muni why he got a good and beautiful wife. The Muni replied that somehow, for some reason, he observed the vrata of Vaishakh month for the last five days. So he got a good wife and also the Brahmin birth. Then the Muni advised him to observe austerity at least for last seven days of Vaishakh month, with devotion to Lord Krishna.

Since that Brahmin observed the *vrata* of Vaishakh month for at least the left out seven days, he got sons, he became rich, ultimately he got love of Godhead and went back to the spiritual world!

SIGNIFICANCE

On this day, bathing in the holy Ganga or in some other rivers is also considered to be of high religious merit. It is on this day that the portals of Sri Badrinarain in the Himalayas open after long snowy winter. Devotees worship Lord Badrinarain on this day with offering of food and other things, either at home or temples.

CELEBRATIONS

On this day fast is observed and Vishnu, along with his consort Lakhmi, is worshipped with the offerings of holy Ganga water, *tulsi* (basil) leaves, incense, flowers, lamps, new raiments and *naivedya*. The Brahmins are given food grains and other foodstuff in charity.

Ashokashthami

Chaitra Shukla Ashthami is also celebrated as Ashokashthami in Orissa. A car festival of Lingaraj at Bhubaneshwar is held on the pattern of the car festival of Lord Jagannath at Puri. The idol of Lord Lingaraj is taken out in a giant wooden chariot to Rameshwar temple, about two kms from the Lingaraj temple and returns after a four-day stay there. It is a major local festival and witnessed by thousands of devotees and spectators.

Baisakhi

On the memorable Baisakhi day of March 30 of A.D. 1699, Guru Gobind Singh called a big meeting at Kesgarh Sahib near Anandpur Sahib. Between fifty to eighty thousand Sikhs attended this meeting. When all were expecting to hear words of comfort and consolation from the lips of their Guru, they were perturbed to see him with a drawn sword in his hand who cried, 'Is there anyone here who would lay down his life for *Dharam?*' There was utter silence, but the Guru went on repeating his demand.

At the third call Daya Ram, a Khatri of Lahore, rose from his seat and offered himself. The Guru took him into an adjoining enclosure....(and soon after) came out with the (blood) dripping....(sword in hand) and, flourishing it before the gathering, he asked again, 'Is there any other Sikh here who will offer himself as a sacrifice(for the cause of *Dharam*)? At this, Dharam Das, a Jat of Delhi, came forward and he too was taken into the enclosure....(The Guru again came out with the blood-stained sword, and repeated his previous demand).

In the same way three other men stood up, one after another, and offered themselves for the sacrifice: One was Mohkam Chand, a washerman of Dwarka (Gujarat state); another was Himmat, a cook of Jagannath (Orissa state); and the third was Sahib Chand, a barber of Bidar (Karnataka state). The Guru, after dressing the five in handsome clothes, brought them back to the assembly.

These five were then administered sweetened water (*amrit*). They were then knighted as *Panj Piaras*, the five beloved ones, the first members of the order of the Khalsa. The Guru then asked them to administer the *Pahul* to him in the same manner in which he had given the *Pahul* to them, and it was done so.

With the creation of the order of the Khalsa, the *panth* created history and since then, the history of Punjab has been the history of Sikhs. Baisakhi played a significant role in this regard.

In 1762, Ahmed Shah Abdali, with the sole purpose to destroy the entire Sikh race, declared '*Jehad*'(holy-war) against the Sikhs and all the Muslims of the Punjab rallied under this slogan. The Sikhs were surrounded near Kup village in Ludhiana district. Chronicles mention that about twenty thousand Sikhs were martyred in a single day. This event is known in the history of the Sikhs as "Ghallughara" (Bloody Carnage). After this, Ahmed Shah Abdali thought that he had crushed the entire Sikh nation, but was greatly disillusioned when after a few months, he heard that the Sikhs in large numbers were celebrating Baisakhi at Amritsar. Baisakhi reminds every Sikh of his cultural and religious heritage. On Baisakhi day all the Sikhs used to assemble at Amritsar and discuss their problems relating to politics and religion. This convention still goes

The celebrations of Baisakhi are similar to the three-day schedule of the celebrations of other Gurparabs. It is generally celebrated on 13th April every year.

SIGNIFICANCE

Baisakhi also marks the beginning of a month-long Vaisakh bathing. The pilgrimage to the holy shrine of Badrinath in the Himalayas also commences from this day. The charities done during the month of Vaisakh are believed to earn great religious merit, and so people generously give money, grains and other things to the poor, needy and the Brahmins; and observe fast, chant the glories of the Lord and practise such other pious activities.

CELEBRATIONS

On this day people bathe in sacred tanks, rivers pools or near the wells early in the morning; dress themselves in festive clothes and visit shrines, temples and gurudwaras to offer prayers and worship.

It is a north Indian festival, but especially in Punjab it is celebrated with great enthusiasm and fervour. The people of Punjab perform *Bhangra* dance, *Gidda* dance, sing folk songs to the tune of drum-beats, exchange greetings, enjoy feasts and such other merry-making with gay abandon. People celebrate this day by visiting gurudwaras and distributing *karah prasad*.

Bihu

The breathtaking hills and valleys of Assam come alive with the sound of Bihu thrice a year. A festival that marks the change of season, Bihu is accompanied both by piety and great rejoicing. One of the seven north-eastern states of India (which are also known as the Seven Sisters), Assam is renowned for its picturesque landscape, exotic fauna and fun-loving people.

ORIGIN OF THE FESTIVAL

Originating in the pre-Aryan days around 3500 B.C., the festival of Bihu used to last for a whole month, though nowadays work pressure has reduced it to a week. A no-holds-barred dancing session is the most intriguing part of the festival and symbolizes the fertility rites of the original inhabitants of the hilly regions of the northeast in India. The farmers fancied that the erotic content of the songs would sexually arouse the earth's body, leading to an abundant harvest.

Bihag Bihu or Rangoli Bihu, the first of the three Bihus, is celebrated in the month of April on the dates coinciding with the Sankranti, Chait or Baisak (13th, 14th and 15th April).

ASSAMESE NEW YEAR

According to the solar calendar that the Assamese follow, the New Year usually falls on 14th April. Brilliantly-coloured flowers and luxuriant foliage dress the whole of Assam in all the hues of the rainbow during the month of April. An abundance of *kopoful* (orchids), mostly purple in colour, in unusual shapes and sizes dot the trees, and the *bhebel* creepers are in full bloom creating an enchanting kaleidoscope of colours. No one can fault the Assamese for their choice of seasons for the Bihu festivals.

The vivid attire of the Assamese youth and the colourful accessories like *kopoful* adorning the hair of the young lasses blend with the hues of nature, spreading joy and good cheer. The day is marked with dancing, though restricted exclusively to men, who participate with unbridled enthusiasm and energy. But the winds of change have blown through this remote state also. Surrendering to contemporary trends, youngsters gather in the town centre and learn the steps from an old hand much in demand on this day.

GOMACHA WEAVING FOR DANCE

Assamese women are experts at weaving the *gomacha*, a towel with intricately woven designs, ceremonially presented as Bihu (Bihu presents) to the men of the family. A young girl too may gift these beautiful souvenirs on Bihu as a token of love. Young lads love to flaunt their prizes by tying them around their waist or as headbands while dancing. But things start warming up as the *Bihu Dals* approach. Now a few words about the *Bihu Dals*. They are wandering minstrels who come visiting through the week, dancing and singing devotional songs (*hosari*) in praise of Lord Krishna (the black god of the

Hindus), invoking his blessings for health, wealth and happiness.

GARUR BIHU

The first day or Garur Bihu, also called *Uraka*, falls on the day of Sankranti and is devoted to the cow that is considered to be a sacred animal in India. The rationale behind the worshipping of cows is very simple. They are the greatest assets of a farmer because not only do they produce milk but this species also help plough fields, transport men, crop and so on. A lot of tender, loving care is showered on cows on this day, starting with bathing them in the pond. The horns and hooves are brushed with whisks made from *deegloti* or *makheatr* (lilsoca salocrfolea).

A mixture of twigs, turmeric and *moong dal* (pulse) acts as a disinfectant, and is applied as a paste. A hearty meal of gourd and brinjal is fed to the cows after which their foreheads are marked with vermilion. As the night falls, the tired but satiated cows are led back to their sheds and thoroughly cleansed. Only then does the household sit down for a sumptuous meal of assorted preparations of *chirwa* (flat rice) and a mind-boggling array of sweets.

GABHORI BIHU

The third day of the festival is the Gabhori Bihu and is earmarked as the day for young ladies. The fair maidens of Assam look gorgeous in their *muga* silk wear and ornate *gumkham* bracelets. The orchids adorning the hair of the ladies add a whimsical touch to the formality of the outfit. Swaying to the beat of the *toka* (drum) and *gogona* (made from bamboo held between the teeth), the women dance the night away amidst the gentle breeze under the banyan trees. Couplets are created spontaneously. Starting with a slow tempo, the rhythm builds up to a crescendo.

KATI BIHU

The second Bihu named Kati Bihu or Kangali Bihu is held in the month of Kartik (September or October). But there is a world of difference in the celebration of this Bihu from the former.

Slowly but surely, winter is approaching, heralding the season for sowing seeds.

This is a solemn occasion as people worship the deities for a rich harvest. The young learn to value hard work so that they do not squander money away.

MAGH BIHU

The Magh Bihu that generally falls on January 14, on the Sankranti of the month, is the third Bihu that calls for a grand celebration in Assamese homes. This is again a joyous occasion as the granaries are stocked with the recently harvested crop. Seven days of non-stop fun and frolic mark this festival. But the special thing about this Bihu is the elaborate and sumptuous cuisine that is prepared. This grand feast known as *bhog* is held on the night of the first day of the festival that is also called *Uruka*.

Buddha Purnima

Bhagwan Buddha was born at Lumbini in Nepal, attained enlightenment at Uruvela, near Bodh Gaya, in Bihar and finally *moksha* at Kusinagar, in the country of Mallas, now in Uttar Pradesh, on this very day, i.e., Vaishakh Purnima (the full moon day of Vaisakh; April-May). The association of the same day with three great events of Buddha's life has made it the most important festival of the Buddhist world.

HISTORY

The belief and practice of Buddhism dates back to the time of Prince Siddharth Gautam, who was born in the southern Terai region of the country in about 563 BC. Till he was 29, the young prince led a very sheltered life in the royal palace of his father. He was completely unaware of the tragedies of everyday life.

One day, he convinced his charioteer to take him outside the walls of his palace and he was shocked to see the sight of an old man, a cripple and a corpse. The realisation that there was more to life than the lavish and luxurious life he was leading, made him abandon all the worldly pleasures and search for enlightenment and the true meaning of life.

After much wandering and searching, Gautam finally attained enlightenment while meditating under a Banyan tree. The enlightenment took place in Gautama's thirty-sixth year. Henceforth, known as the "*Buddha*" or "*the enlightened one*", he began to preach to all who would listen to his concept of "*The Four Noble Truths*" and an "*Eightfold Path*" of discipline to achieve perfect bliss.

CELEBRATIONS

Buddha Purnima is celebrated in regions under the influence of Buddhism, with immense piety, devotion and fervour. Special celebrations are held at places like Sarnath, Sanchi, Kusinagar and Bodh Gaya. In the Deer Park at Sarnath, near Varanasi, he preached for the first time and turned the *Wheel of Dharma*. At Sanchi some of his sacred remains are enshrined under a magnificent *stupa*.

RITUAL

Prayers are sung and the Buddhists offer worship in all the major Buddhist shrines such as Swayambhunath and Boudhnath. At Swayambhunath, for example, millions of devout Buddhists gather to chant prayers and to burn butter lamps. The next morning a giant figure of Lord Buddha is displayed to all the followers and hundreds of small shrines are visited and worshipped.

Large groups of people parade through the streets praising the Lord and his teachings. Special flags, usually red, blue, yellow and white can be seen flying high above all the Buddhist households.

PROCESSION

On this day, images and portraits of Buddha are taken out in a procession. Devotees of Buddha recite and read the sacred scriptures, observe fast, worship Buddha at home and in temples, and practise charity.

SIGNIFICANCE

We find that Buddha's teachings are even more relevant today. He preached that this world is full of sorrows because of our attachment to materialistic world. Our sufferings are the direct result of our desires. According to him it is our desires that result in reincarnations and a ceaseless chain of rebirths, suffering, sickness, old age and death. Extinction of desire and attachment is essential for salvation, and the only way is to follow the *Eightfold Path* : Right Belief, Right Intention, Right Word, Right Conduct, Right Living, Right Efforts, Right Thinking and Right Meditation. He underlined the importance of striking a balance between indulgence and asceticism, and this is what most of the people badly need today.

Chaitra Festival

The Meenakshi temple is said to have been originally founded by Indra himself. The legend goes that once Indra set out on a pilgrimage to expiate the misdeeds he had done inadvertently. During his pilgrimage when he came near Madurai, he felt the burden of his misdeeds suddenly taken off and he found a Shiva Lingam there. He ascribed this miracle to the Lingam and immediately constructed a temple there and enshrined the Lingam. Indra performed a *puja* in the temple as a result of which Lord Shiva himself caused the golden lotuses to appear in the nearby pool. Indra was overwhelmed with joy. This took place on Chaitra Purnima. The golden lotus lake is still present in the temple premises.

CELEBRATIONS

In Madurai, a great festival celebrating the marriage of Lord Sundareshwara with Goddess Meenakshi is held with great religious enthusiasm in the month of Chaitra (March-April). It lasts for 10 days and is focussed on the Meenakshi temple, an extraordinary example of the Dravidian architecture. The deities are taken around the temple several times. Thousands of devotees from all over India gather here on this occasion. The wedding anniversary is known as *Meenakshi-kalyanam*, which is the most spectacular festival of Madurai.

Chaitra Parva

The tribals in Orissa celebrate Chaitra Parva on the full moon day of the month of Chaitra. It starts eight days before the Purnima. The celebration is marked by fasting, dancing and hunting by tribals. The head of the family pays homage to his forefathers in the presence of the village priest called '*Jyani*', and every member of the family attends it in new festive costumes. They start eating mangoes of the fresh crop only from the day of this festival onwards. *Danda Nach* and *Chaitighoda Nach* (two folk dance forms) are also performed on this occasion. Animal sacrifice is one of the main features of the festival.

Chaitra Purnima

The full moon day of Chaitra (March-April) is also observed as a sacred day in honour of Chitra Gupta in South India.

HISTORY AND SIGNIFICANCE

On this day, Chitra Gupta, the assistant of god Dharmaraj in heaven, is worshipped. It is Chitra Gupta who maintains the accounts of our good and bad actions in this world, and we are rewarded or punished accordingly in the afterlife. At Kanchipuram, the image of god Chitra Gupta is taken out in a procession and the devotees take a holy dip in the river Chitra flowing down the nearby hills.

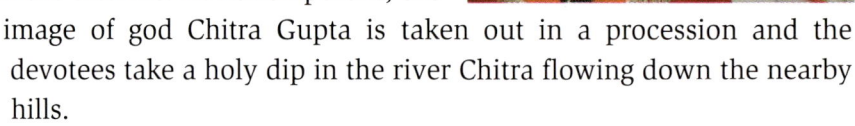

CELEBRATIONS

The worship and prayer offered to Chitra Gupta, the chief divine scribe, makes us aware that the gods high above are keeping a watch on each and every action of ours and maintaining a record of it. It helps us in self-analysis and maintaining a good conduct so as to reap good rewards and avoid punishment after death. It also reminds us that a sin can be forgiven if one repents sincerely, vows not to repeat it, and prays to the Lord with penitent heart, devotion and intense faith. A metal or an earthen pitcher filled with water is worshipped with an elaborate ritual so as to invoke the deity. Chitra Gupta literally means 'hidden picture' and it is he who, after our death, presents a true picture of our actions during our lifetime.

Chandan Yatra

The summer festival of Lord Jagannath is celebrated with much religious zeal and passion at Puri in Orissa. The Chandan Yatra of Jagannath begins on Akshya Tritiya (the third day of bright half of Baisakh) falling in April and continues for 21 days.

PROCESSION AND CELEBRATIONS

Everyday the representative images of the deities are taken out in grand procession to nearby tanks where they are rowed in profusely decorated boats to the accompaniment of music and dance. On the last day of the celebrations, Bhaund Yatra is performed. This festival is also celebrated at Bhubaneshwar, Baripada and Balanga.

The first period of the 21 days is known as Bahar Chandan. During this period the representative images of Rama, Krishna, Madanmohan, Sridevi and Bhudevi are taken in a procession to Narendra tank. The images of Siva from five Siva temples known as Pancha Pandavas also accompany them to the Narendra tank. At Narendra tank the images are placed in well decorated boats and are worshipped.

The second period known as Bhitar Chandana is celebrated inside the temple. The rites observed during this period are popularly enjoyed.

Cheti Chand
Sindhi New Year Day

Just like Ugadi is the new year in Karnataka and Andhra Pradesh, and Gudi Padwa is the new year day in Maharashtra, Cheti Chand, which falls on the same day, is the Sindhi New Year Day. According to the Hindu calendar, Cheti Chand is celebrated on the first day of the Chaitra month known as *Chet* in Sindhi. Hence it is known as Cheti-Chand. The Sindhi community celebrates the festival of Cheti Chand in honour of the birth of Ishtadeva Uderolal, popularly known as Jhulelal, the patron saint of the Sindhis. This day is considered to be very auspicious and is celebrated with pomp and gaiety. On this day, people worship water – the elixir of life. Followers of

Jhulelal observe *Chaliho Sahab* – suggestive of the forty long days and nights they underwent rituals and vigil on the banks of Sindhu. They did not shave, nor did they wear new clothes or shoes. They did not use soap or oil or any opulent thing. They just washed their clothes, dried them and wore them again. In the evening, they worshipped god Varun, sang songs in his praise and prayed for their solace and salvation. After 40 days of *Chaliho*, the followers of Jhulelal celebrated the occasion with festivity as 'thanks-giving day', a ritual practised even today.

A lamp is lit on a bronze plate, and this ritual is called Jyot Jagan. One lamp, *akshaoil* and vermilion are kept on this plate. A procession is taken out to the river front or seashore. Lakhs of people participate in the long processions taken out in different cities, with colourful floats depicting the life of the saint and other aspects of Sindhi culture. The Sindhi folk dance called "*Chhej*" is performed with the procession. People go to a river or a lake and Bahrano Saheb is immersed in the water along with rice and sugar *prasad* called "*Akho*". It is customary to sing Lal Sain's *Panjras* and *Palav* to seek his grace. New ventures are started on this day. After the worship of Jhulelal, the Sindhi community display and present their rich culture through dance, drama, music and folk arts.

Legend of Jhulelal–Mirkhshah, a tyrant and a fanatic, forced Hindus to embrace Islam. The oppressed Hindus prayed and underwent rituals and vigil on the banks of Sindhu. In the evening, they worshipped god Varun, sang songs in his praise and prayed for their solace and salvation. No new clothes or shoes were worn. Men did not shave. And finally on the 40th day, the river god spoke to them. The answer to the prayers of Hindus was Jhulelal. He was born to Devaki and Ratanchand of Nasarpur on Cheti Chand, two *tithis* from new moon of *Chet*. A Punjabi astrologer in Nasarpur called the child Uderolal. *Udero* in Sanskrit means one who has sprung from the waters. The inhabitants of Nasarpur called the newborn Amarlal, an immortal child. The cradle of Uderolal would swing on its own, hence the child got the name "*Jhulelal*" which means one who swings. As a child, Uderolal performed many miracles for Ratanchand and the inhabitants of Nasarpur. Mirkhshah became very anxious to have first-hand knowledge about the mysterious child, as divine interventions always led to the defeat of Mirkshah in his attempts to convert people. Finally when Uderolal came face to face with Mirkhshah, he said,"Whatever you see around yourself is the creation of the one and only God, whom you call '*Allah*' and Hindus call '*Ishwar*'. Hindus, Muslims and other human beings are all His creation". Mirkhshah, wavering as usual, was ultimately carried away under pressure of *Maulvies* but, soon, he ordered the arrest of Uderolal. As the officials of the court moved towards Udero, water started flowing in the court. All the courtiers including Mirkhshah found themselves inundated. Simultaneously, fire also broke out. Finally, Mirkhshah realised his mistake and begged of Jhulelal to have mercy on them. Immediately, the fire was blown out on its own and the water receded. The Hindus were saved. Jhulelal thus became the *Asht Dev* of Sindhis.

Gangaur

Gangaur is a festival in which primarily women are the active participants and it is celebrated on the third day of the bright half of Chaitra (February-March).

HISTORY

Goddess Parvati is the symbol of virtue and fidelity and exemplifies all the qualities of a good wife. The word Gangaur signifies the togestherness of Lord Shiva and Parvati. It is believed that during Gangaur, goddess Parvati had returned to her parental home to bless her friends with marital bliss. On the last day of her stay, she was given a grand farewell by her loved ones. Shiva himself arrived to escort his bride Gauri, another name of Parvati, back home.

SIGNIFICANCE

Ramcharit Manas describes Sita's visit to the shrine of Girija or Gauri once, before her marriage, early one morning, accompanied by her lovely companions and attendants, singing joyous songs. After ablutions, Sita approaches the goddess with a cheerful heart and a contemplative mind, and after devoted adoration, she prays to Gauri for a handsome and a perfectly matching groom. And finally her wish is fulfilled when Rama wins her hand in marriage.

PROCESSION

On the final day of Gangaur festival, ladies keep strict fast, worship the goddess, wear colourful raiments and ornaments, exchange sweets, and the wooden or earthen images of Gangaur (Shiva-Parvati) are taken out in procession through the streets for the ceremonial immersion in a nearby lake or tank. A boat procession is taken out on the Pichola Lake in Udaipur.

CELEBRATIONS

It is a great local festival in Rajasthan, and is also celebrated in many parts of northern India with great fervour. Gangaur festival is culminating on the final 18th day of celebrations. The celebrations start right from the next day of Holi with worship and prayers to Gauri – the most fair and benign aspect of Durga, the consort of Shiva.

Both, married women and unmarried girls, worship the goddess every day during the festival with *durva* grass, flowers, fruits and bright brass pots filled with fresh water. The married women seek Gauri's blessings for conjugal happiness and bliss, while the virgins pray for a suitable, handsome husband and future marital prosperity. In Jaipur a sweet dish called *ghewar* is prepared.

Gudi Padava

Gudi Padava is mainly celebrated in Maharashtra on the first day of Chaitra (March-April). Chaitra Pratipada marks the beginning of the Hindu new year. People get up early in the morning, clean up their houses, have ablutions and wear festive and new clothes. Women decorate their houses with *Rangoli*. A silk banner is raised and worshipped and then greetings and sweets are exchanged.

Hanuman Jayanti

On Chaitra Shukla Purnima, i.e. the full moon day of March-April, Hanuman Jayanti is celebrated all over the country. The monkey god Hanuman is worshipped everywhere in India either alone or together with Lord Rama. Hanuman temples dot the entire length and breadth of the country. Every temple dedicated to Rama invariably has an idol of Hanuman. In other temples also the image of Hanuman is found installed.

HISTORY

Hanuman is considered to be one of the greatest embodiments of strength, speed, agility, learning and selfless service to Lord Rama. He could fly at the speed of wind, uproot mountains and trees, assume any size and shape at will and make himself invisible. In the battlefield he became a figure exuding terror, assuming the qualities of colossus, assuming the form of a mountain, or a tall tower, which is invincible. He is depicted with a face red like ruby, skin yellow, coat shining like molten gold and a tail of immense length. He shattered the enemies in the battlefield with his fierce roar. He is considered to be immortal, and this immortality was granted to him by Rama to serve the devotees in distress. His great adventures have been described in great detail and with much reverence in the *Ramayana*.

SIGNIFICANCE

He is considered as the embodiment of *nishkam karmyoga*, love, sincerity and true devotion. Rama and Hanuman are inseparable. His celibacy is of the highest order and he did things which were almost impossible for others, for the sake of Lord Rama. On Hanuman Jayanti, by observing fast, meditating on him and his lord Rama, practising charity, reading the *Hanuman Chaleesa* and spending the day in reciting his glories and adventures, one will be blessed.

We bow to Hanuman, who stand with his palms folded above his forehead, with a flood of tears flowing down his cheeks whenever the names of the Lord is sung.

CELEBRATIONS

The birth anniversary of Hanuman, the son of the wind-god Marut and Anjana Devi, is celebrated with great religious fervour. People visit the shrines dedicated to Lord Hanuman, observe strict fast, offer prayers and *puja*, read the *Ramayana* and the *Hanuman Chaleesa*. On this occasion the idol of Hanuman is given a new coat of vermilion colour mixed with clarified butter and then richly decorated. Fairs are also held at some places near the shrines and charity feasts are also organized.

Janaki Navami

The Janaki Navami fast is observed on the ninth day of the bright half of Baishakh, as she is supposed to have sprung on this day from a furrow, while King Janak was ploughing the field. *Sita* means a furrow. Janak took her up and brought her up as his own child. She is also called '*Ayonija*', not born from the womb. She was actually Sri or Goddess Lakshmi in human form, incarnated in the world for bringing about the ideals of the Indian woman. As an embodiment of self-sacrifice, purity, tenderness, fidelity, conjugal affection and other conceivable female virtues, Sita is par excellence.

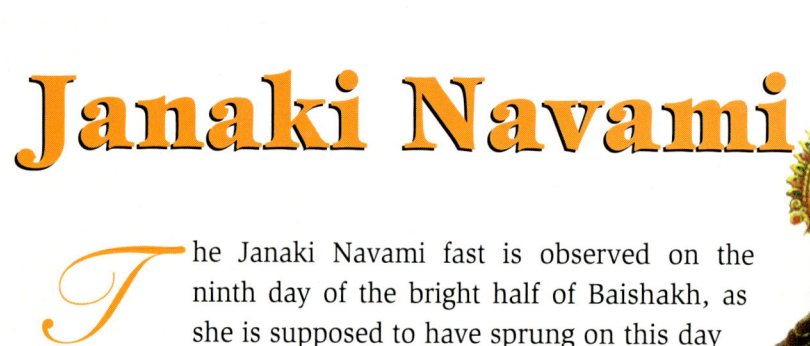

CELEBRATIONS

Some people believe that Sitaji appeared in the field of Janak on the eighth day of the black half of Phalgun, and so they celebrate Janaki Navami on that day. However, observance of fast and offering of prayers and worship to mother Janaki on this auspicious day bestow upon the aspirant conjugal happiness, marital bliss and worldly prosperity.

Mahavir Jayanti

Maharvir Jayanti is the birth anniversary of Lord Mahavir Both the Digambar (sky-clad) and the Shvetambar (white-clad) Jains observe the 13th day of the bright half of the Chaitra month (March-April) as the birth annivesary of Lord Mahavira, the 24th Teerthankara of the Jains and is the main festival of the year. Mahavira, the great teacher and the 24th Tirthankara of Jainism, was the contemporary of Lord Buddha. His mother Trisala or Priyakarini had a series of miraculous dreams heralding the birth of Mahavira. Astrologers interpreting these dreams stated that the child would be either an emperor or Teerthankara Vardhaman achieved enlightenment under an Ashoka tree after two-and-a-half days' fasting and meditation. Then he stripped himself of all his clothes and wore none thereafter, but Shvetambars believe that Indra then presented him a white robe. After his enlightenment he gave away all his wealth and possessions and owned nothing. Mahavira underlined the importance of austerity and complete non-violence as the essential means of spiritual evolution and salvation.

PROCESSION

On this auspicious day grand chariot processions with the images of Mahavira are taken out, rich ceremonies are held in the temples, fasts and charities are observed, Jain scriptures are read, and at some places grand fairs are set up.

CELEBRATIONS

The birth anniversary of Lord Mahavira is celebrated by the entire Jain community throughout the country, but it is celebrated with special charms in Rajasthan and Gujarat, where the Jains are relatively in greater number than in other states. Jain pilgrims from all over the country congregate at the ancient Jain shrines at Girnar and Palitana in Gujarat and at Mahavirji in Rajasthan. Pawapuri and Vaishali in Bihar are other such centres of pilgrimage. Vaishali being his birth place, a grand festival is held there, and it is known as Vaishali Mahotsava.

HINDU FASTS & FESTIVALS

DIGAMBARAS AND SHVETAMBARAS

Around the year 80 AD the Jains split into two sects: Digambaras (space clothed) and Shvetambaras (clothed in white). Digambaras hold that *sadhus* must be naked as a sign of total renunciation. Other doctrines held by the Digambaras but rejected by the Shvetambaras are: 1. Only men can obtain final liberation (*moksha*), women must be reborn as men. 2. The images of the Tirthankars must be represented with downcast eyes, nude and unadorned. 3. Mahavir never married. 4. Once the highest stage of knowledge is reached, a saint can sustain life without eating, and 5. By the 2nd century AD the entire canon of sacred books was lost.

DASH LAXANPARVA

The holiest feast of the Jains is Dashlaxanparva, which is celebrated by the Digambaras from the 5th to the 14th of the bright half of Bhadrapad. During these days there is an atmosphere of joy in every Jain temple. Every day in the morning after taking bath all men and women go to worship in the temple. Then each day there is a lecture on the ten chapters of the holy book "*Shritatvarth.*"

The ten chapters dwell on the following ten duties (*dharma*): 1. *Kshama* (forgiveness), 2. *Mardava* (humility), 3. *Arjava* (simplicity and frankness). 4. *Shaucha* (cleanliness), 5. *Satya* (truthfulness), 6. *Samyama* (self-control), 7. *Tap* (austerity), 8. *Tyag* (renunciation). 9. *Akimchanya* (detachment), and 10. *Bramhacharya* (celibacy). On the day dedicated to "*tyag*" gifts are offered to social service institutions, and on the first day of the dark half of *Ashvin*, at the end of the celebration, all the men come together and embracing each other they ask pardon for the offences committed during the past year.

The 14th day of the bright half of Bhadrapad is known as *Anant Chaturdashi* (endless fourteenth). This is a very important day for the Jains, being the last day of the *Dashlaxanparva*. According to Jain scriptures one can gain much merit by observing a vow on this day. The Jains of the *Shvetambara* sect celebrate the *Paryushan* feast, from the 12th of the dark half of Bhadrapad to the 4th of the bright half of Ashvin.

"Ahimsa" or "non-hurting" of life is the main principle of Jainism.

"Even unintentionally and the involuntary stepping on an ant may have serious consequences for the soul... Not only living things, but everything in nature must be respectfully treated."

"There is no place for God in Jainism, which has constructed a complicated theory of '*karma*' and *karmic* matter. *Karma* is that general energy of the soul that causes its attachment to matter and its subsequent defilement, a kind of link between matter and spirit.

Rama Naumi

Rama Naumi, the birthday of Lord Rama, falls on the ninth day of the bright half of the month of Chaitra (March-April).

SIGNIFICANCE

Rama, the seventh incarnation of Vishnu, was born to King Dashratha and Queen Kaushalya of Ayodhya during the *Tretayuga*. He was the eldest son of the king but, under a subtle plan by his younger queen, Rama was sent to exile for fourteen years. During the exile, he was accompanied by his wife Sita and brother Laxman. It was also during this period of exile that Sita was abducted by Ravana and Rama defeated him in the war and got Sita back. After returning to Ayodhya, Rama was coronated and he proved to be a role model of a righteous king and an ideal husband and is known as *Maryada Purushottam*, the righteous and the supreme one.

CELEBRATIONS

Idol of Rama is decorated and worshipped in the temples or at homes, *Vedic* hymns chanted, fast observed with only fruits being eaten. These celebrations are usually done for nine days, culminating on Rama Naumi, the ninth day.

LEGEND

Legend has it that Lord Vishnu appeared on earth at the end of *Tretayuga*, the second age of the world, to give lessons in righteousness, to humankind and to kill Ravana, the ten-headed demon king of Lanka. He also curtailed Parashuram's ambitions against Kshatriyas. Goddess Lakshmi also incarnated herself as Sita to remain close to him.

HINDU FASTS & FESTIVALS

Shankaracharya Jayanti

The birth anniversary of Adi Shankaracharya is celebrated on the fifth day of the bright half of Baishakh in the south. But in north India, it is celebrated on the tenth day.

HISTORY AND SIGNIFICANCE

Shankaracharya has been one of the greatest saint philosophers of India, and also symbolizes India's cultural and emotional integrity and unity.

His teachings were a great boon and blessing to millions of Hindu souls, who were then groping in the darkness of ignorance and religious decay and disintegration. He is believed to be the incarnation of Shiva himself. He revived Brahmanism and took *Vedanta* philosophy to a new height. He is believed to have lived between A.D. 788 and 820. He was a native of Malabar, in Kerala. He worked many miracles and died at an early age of thirty two. He is reputed of authoring many original philosophical works and commentaries on the *Upanishads*, *Vedanta Sutras* and the *Bhagvad Gita*. He has rightly been designated as our 'Vedanta Guru'. His philosophy is equally accessible both to the learned and the layman. He composed many beautiful hymns, and wanted people to devote themselves to God in any of his forms or incarnations.

CELEBRATIONS

Shankaracharya Jayanti is a fit occasion to study his works, to fast, to meditate and to rededicate oneself to the service of the Lord and the country. His teachings are a form of blessing and a guiding spirit to his followers.

Sheetala Ashthami

Sheetala Ashthami, as the name itself indicates, is observed on the eighth day of the bright half of Chaitra (March-April) in honour of goddess Sheetala.

SIGNIFICANCE

Sheetala is the goddess of smallpox and her blessings are invoked for protection against this dreaded disease. Sheetala is depicted as roaming in the countryside, riding on an ass. She is identified with Devi or Durga in her role as goddess of smallpox.

CELEBRATIONS

On this day, which falls either on Monday or Friday, the womenfolk visit the shrine of Sheetala in the morning and after ablutions, make offerings of rice, home-made sweets, cooked food and holy water mixed with milk. At several places colourful fairs are held on this occasion near the shrine of Sheetala and there is a lot of merry-making, singing, dancing, feasting and brisk buying and selling.

Ugadi Parva

Ugadi is the beginning of the Telugu new year. It marks the onset of spring, of new life and new beginning. On the first day of the Chaitra month this festival is observed with gaiety and enthusiasm and people visit each other, enjoy feasts and wear new clothes. This day is considered auspicious and new ventures are started. The festive day begins with ritual bath and prayers continue till late night. The *purohit* makes predictions by reading the almanac.

HISTORY

It is believed that Brahma created the world on this very day. Lord Vishnu is also said to have incarnated himself as *Matsya* (the fish incarnation) on this day. Brahma is the prominent deity worshipped on this day.

SIGNIFICANCE

It is believed that the creator of the Hindu pantheon Lord Brahma started creation on this day – *Chaitra suddha padhyami* or the *Ugadi* day. Also the great Indian mathematician Bhaskaracharya's calculations proclaimed the Ugadi day from the sun-rise on as the beginning of the new year, new month and new day. It marks the beginning of new life with plants acquiring new roots, shoots and leaves. Spring is considered the first season of the year. The vibrancy of life with verdent fields, meadows full of colourful blossoms signifies growth, prosperity and well-being.

CELEBRATIONS

Preparations for the festival begin a week ahead. Houses are given a thorough wash. Shopping for new clothes and buying other items that go with the requirements of the festival are done with a lot of excitement.

On Ugadi day, people wake up before the dawn and take a head bath after which they decorate the entrance of their houses with fresh mango leaves. People also splash fresh cow dung water on the ground in front of their house and draw colourful floral designs. This is a common sight in every household. People perform the ritualistic worship to God invoking his blessings before they start off with the new year. They pray for their health, wealth and prosperity and success in business too.

Ugadi is celebrated with festive fervour in Maharashtra, Karnataka and Andhra Pradesh. While it is called Ugadi in A.P. and Karnataka, in Maharashtra it is known as "*Gudipadava*".

The celebration of Ugadi is marked by religious zeal and social merriment. Special dishes are prepared for the occasion. In Andhra Pradesh, eatables such as "*Pulihora*", "*Bobbatlu*" and preparations made with raw mango go well with the occasion. In Karnataka too, similar preparations are made but called "*Puliogure*" and "*Holige*". The Maharashtrians make "*Puran Poli*" or sweet *rotis*.

UGADI PACHCHADI

It is a season for raw mangoes spreading its aroma in the air and the fully blossomed neem tree that makes the air healthy. Also, jaggery made with fresh crop of sugarcane adds a renewed flavour to the typical dishes associated with Ugadi.

"*Ugadi pachchadi*" is one such dish that has become synonymous with Ugadi. It is made of new jaggery, raw mango pieces and neem flowers and new tanarind which truly reflect life – a combination of sweet, sour and bitter tastes!

Vishu

The festival of Vishu is celebrated with joy and mirth on the first day of Malayalam month of Medam. This corresponds to the month of April-May according to Gregorian calendar. The occasion holds a lot of significance for Hindus as Vishu marks the astronomical new year day.

The traditional people of Kerala practise a lot of colorful rituals and customs on Vishu. Most of these traditions are based on a belief that Vishu must be celebrated well as the good things of the first day of the new year will continue for the rest of the year too.

RITUALS AND TRADITIONS

Most important ritual of the day is called 'Kani Kanal', the literal translation of this is 'first sight'. In *Kani Kanal* there is a prescribed list of items which a person must see as first thing on the Vishu morning to bring good luck. This includes gold ornaments, fresh white cloth, a measure of rice or paddy, flowers of the *Konna* tree (Cussia fistula), halved jack fruits, halved coconuts and yellow cucumber. All these things are kept in a big vessel (*thali*) and behind the vessel (*thali*) is kept a bell metal mirror and a garlanded deity of Lord Krishna. Two standing oil lamps are also placed before the deity.

Preparations of *Kani* are done a night before by the lady of the house. Master of the house is the first person to see *Kani* and then the other family members follow. Children are brought blindfolded from their rooms to see *Kani Kanal*, *Vishu Kani* is later distributed amongst the poor and needy people. Reason behind this ritual is the strong belief of the people that the fortune of the rest of the year depends on the first object they see on the Vishu day. There is also a tradition to give small amounts of cash to children of the family. This tradition is called *Vishu Kaineetam*. People believe that this custom will ensure prosperity for their children in future.

A large number of people prefer to see *Vishu Kani* in temples. A huge rush of devotees can be seen in the temples of Guruvayur, Ambalapuzha and Sabarimala where special prayers are organised to mark the day. People stay overnight in the courtyards of these temples a night before Vishu so that they see *Kani*, first *darshan* in the temple. Devotees close their eyes and set their eyes on *Kani* and deity so that when the doors to the deity open early in the morning, the first thing they see is *Kani*.

CELEBRATIONS

A grand *sadya* (feast) is prepared by women of the house and the whole family sits together at lunch to relish it. Dishes are usually prepared from jackfruits, mangoes, pumpkins, and gourds besides other vegetables and fruits, which are in plenty at that time of the season. People also wear *kodi vastram* (new clothes) on this day. *Patakkams* (firecrackers) are burst in the midst of dancing and merry-making to mark the day.

A group of young men and women dress up as '*chozhi*', wearing a skirt of dried banana leaves and masks on their faces and go from house to house in the village dancing and collecting small amounts of money. On Vishu, these entertainers get good rewards for their performances. The money is spent on the *Vishuwela* (the new year fair).

Guru Purnima

It is also known as Vyas Purnima, and the day is dedicated to the Guru, because Rishi Vyas himself was a great Guru. Vyas or Veda-Vyas, the son of Rishi Parashar and Satyavati, is also known as Krishna Dwaipayna, because he was dark complexioned and was born on an island or *dwipa*. He is said to have compiled the four *Vedas*, the *Mahabharata* and the eighteen *Purans*.

This day reminds the story of a devoted student Eklavya, and the matchless Nishad archer youth, who gladly gave his right hand thumb as *dakshina* (reward) to his relentless *guru* and teacher Dronacharya. He gave it too gladly. Eklavya is one of the greatest examples of devotion to the teacher, and it is appropriate that he is remembered on this day.

SIGNIFICANCE

The full moon day of Ashadh is well known all over the country as 'Guru Vyas or Ashadh Purnima'. This festival dates back to time immemorial. This auspicious day is set apart for the veneration and worship of the *Guru*. In ancient days the students or *brahmcharis* used to get their education in *Ashrams* and *Gurukuls*. The students would worship their teachers on this day and pay them their *Gurudakshina* (fee and presents) according to their means and capacity. The devotees and disciples fast on this day and worship their *gurus* for seeking their blessings.

Jyaishtha Ashthami

This festival is celebrated on the eighth day of the bright half of Jyaishtha (May-June) at Kheer Bhawani, in Kashmir. To celebrate this birthday festival of the goddess, people from the adjoining hill areas assemble in large numbers at the shrine and offer prayers and worship at the lotus feet of the goddess. *Kheer* (rice boiled in milk) is prepared on this day as a *naivedya* (food offering). The hill-folk sing hymns and songs in praise of Bhawani.

Kheer Bhawani is the personal goddess of the Kashmiri Hindus and hundreds of them visit the shrine daily. This beautiful marble shrine stands amidst a pool, formed by spring waters, which change their colours into rosy red, turquoise green, pale lemon, sky blue, milky white or pure white from time to time. The temple is situated 25 kms, from Srinagar, and 5 kms from Ganderbal.

Nirjala Ekadashi

Nirijala Ekadashi is an important Ekadashi among the twenty-four Ekadashis falling in one year.

Ekadashi is considered to be a very sacred day and so a fast is observed on every eleventh day of the bright and dark half of the moon.

SIGNIFICANCE

The eleventh day of the moon is especially set apart for devotional activities and fasting. It is a day dedicated to the worship of Vishnu. *Vishnu Puran* and *Markandeya Puran* give detailed description of the benefits resulting from the observance of *Ekadashi vrata*. It is believed that Lord Vishnu transformed himself into Ekadashi to redeem the mankind from sins. This day is significant as it is considered to be the embodiment of Lord Hari himself.

CELEBRATIONS

In all, 24 Ekadashi fasts are observed in a year, but there are some Ekadashis which are relatively of greater significance. Nirjala Ekadashi is one of these. Not only people refrain from taking food on this day but even the intake of water is impermissible. Both men and women observe strict fast and offer *puja* to Vishnu to ensure happiness, prosperity and forgiveness of transgressions and sins. On the preceding day – that is on the 10th lunar day; *Sandhya vandan* is performed and only one meal is taken. In the evening Vishnu is worshipped holding some *durva* grass in the hand. The night is spent in meditation and prayer. On the day of Ekadashi eating rice is totally prohibited.

During the Nirjala Ekadashi, *Panchamrat* is prepared by mixing together milk, ghee, curd, honey and sugar, and then offered to the image of Vishnu or poured over the Shaligram. Then the deity is adorned with rich raiments, ornaments and jewels and a fan is placed beside it. Then Vishnu is meditated upon as the Supreme Lord of the universe and *puja* is done with flowers, lamps, water, incense, etc.

The faithful observance of the fast and other rituals on this day ensures happiness, salvation, longevity and prosperity. After completion of the worship and rituals clothes, grains, umbrellas, fans, pitchers filled with water, etc. are given in charity to the Brahmins according to one's means and capacity. The month of Jyaishtha is very hot and the days are long, and so observing fast, without even taking a drop of water from dawn to dusk means a great act of piety and austerity. Ekadashi vow and vigil enhances mental equipoise, tolerance and spiritual powers and grants great religious merit.

Rath Yatra

The legend of the origin of Lord Jagannath is equally fantastic. A hunter named Jara in ignorance killed Krishna, and Krishna's body was left to rot under a tree, but some pious travellers found his bones and placed them in a box. Later on, Vishnu directed a devout king Indradyumna in a dream to make an image of Jagannath and to place the bones of Krishna inside it. Vishwakarma, the architect of the gods, was assigned the job of making the image. He agreed to make the image, on the condition that he should be left undisturbed till the work was complete. A fortnight passed and the king grew impatient and entered the place to see the images, which made Vishwakarma angry, and he left the images unfinished. That is why the deities have neither hands nor feet. Indradyumna prayed to Brahma, who promised to make the image famous. Brahma gave the images eyes and soul and also acted as the high priest at the consecration ceremony.

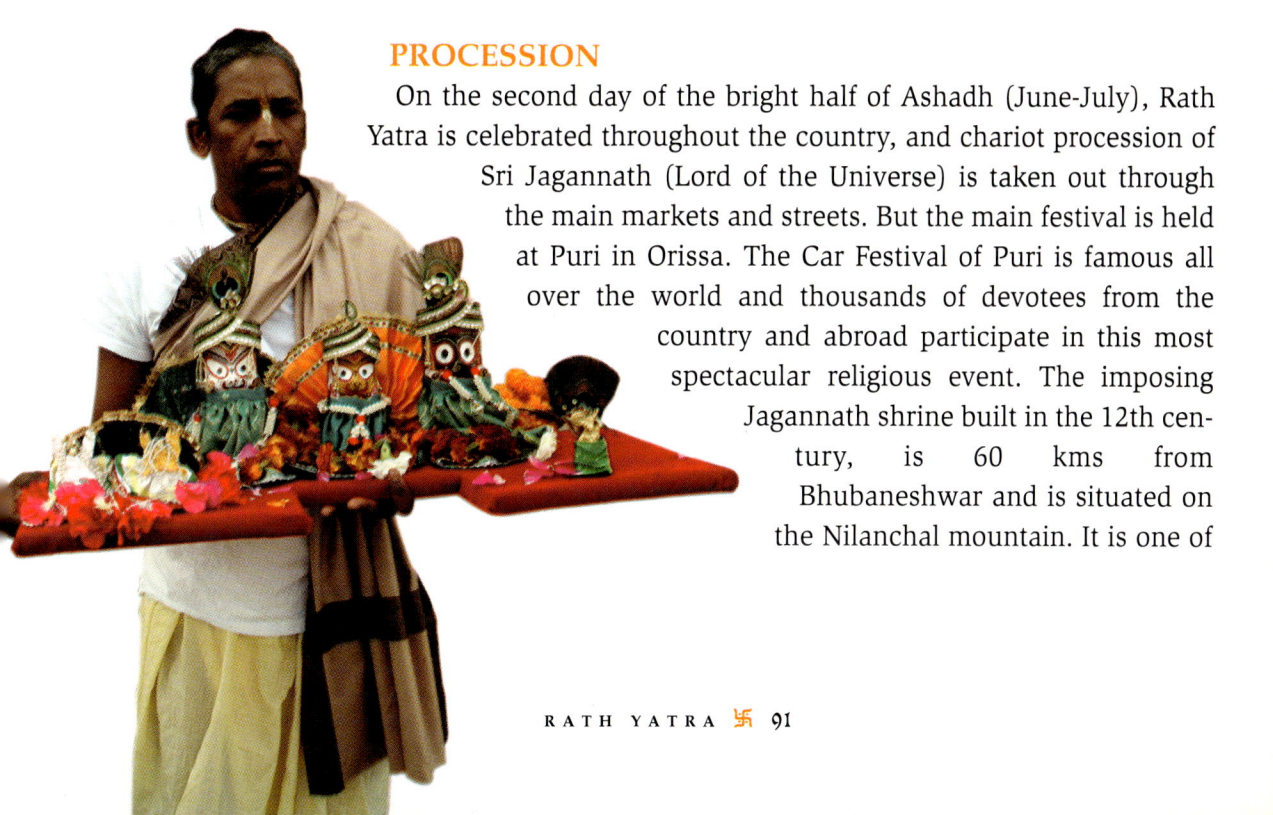

PROCESSION

On the second day of the bright half of Ashadh (June-July), Rath Yatra is celebrated throughout the country, and chariot procession of Sri Jagannath (Lord of the Universe) is taken out through the main markets and streets. But the main festival is held at Puri in Orissa. The Car Festival of Puri is famous all over the world and thousands of devotees from the country and abroad participate in this most spectacular religious event. The imposing Jagannath shrine built in the 12th century, is 60 kms from Bhubaneshwar and is situated on the Nilanchal mountain. It is one of the four great seats of pilgrimage in India. The other three are Badrinath, Dwarka and Rameshwaram.

For a devout Hindu, a pilgrimage to Jagannath Puri is a must and a lifelong ambition. It is believed that three days and nights of sojourn to Puri will free a pilgrim from future births and deaths. Most of the time it is crowded with pilgrims, but on the occasion of Rath Yatra, Puri becomes a seething ocean of humanity. On this auspicious day Lord Jagannath is taken out in a huge procession on an enormous chariot, with a height of 45 feet, breadth of 35 square feet, and supported on 16 wheels, 7 feet in diameter. The chariot is drawn by thousands of devotees who vie with one another to have this honour.

The other two chariots are those of Balbhadra and Subhadra, brother and sister of Sri Krishna. Balbhadra's chariot is 44 feet high and has 14 wheels, while that of Subhadra is 43 feet high and has 12 wheels. The event commemorates Krishna's journey to Mathura from Gokul at Kansa's invitation. The chariot procession goes along the broad avenue to Gundicha Mandir, the lord's summer garden house, where they stay for seven days and then are brought back to the temple. At the termination of the ceremony the chariots are broken up to create religious relics. Every year new chariots are made. The deities themselves are made of wood and renewed at certain intervals as per conditions satisfied by astrological calculations. The woods used to make the images should also satisfy certain conditions. During the past one and half centuries the images were remade in 1863, 1893, 1931,1950, 1969 and 1977. An outstanding feature of the temple is that no caste distinction is applicable over there. All are equal whether one happens to be a Brahmin or a Chandal or a Shudra.

The other festival celebrated here with great fervour is the bathing festival or *Snan Yatra* held in the month of Jyaishtha. But Rath Yatra is the most fantastic and captivating annual event.

CELEBRATIONS

The Rath Yatra is a community festival. There are no *pujas* in individual homes, nor is there any fasting.

In the temple kitchen, a special chamber is set apart for working of *Mahaprasad* consisting of *dal*, rice, *saag*, curd and *kheer*. A portion is taken out as offering for the gods. It is sold to the pilgrims on banana leaves at nominal cost. Jagannath temple is affectionately called the largest hotel in the world. Its kitchen has space to cook 72 quintals of rice daily to feed a lakh people. 400 cooks are engaged for the purpose.

SIGNIFICANCE

The king of Puri, the descendant of King Anantavarman Chodaganga, the original founder of the temple, alone has the right to carry the Lord's umbrella and other paraphernalia, and it is he who sweeps the path before the chariots. Over 6,000 male adults are in the Lord's service, headed by one chief. A total of around 20,000 people are said to be dependent on the temple for their livelihood. The Jagannath temple is a different world in itself. The festival is observed all over the country where there is a temple dedicated to Lord Jagannath.

Snan Yatra
Bathing Festival

On Jyaishtha Purnima (full moon day of May-June) a grand bathing festival is held in Orissa. On this auspicious occasion the images of Lord Jagannath –Balbhadra, Subhadra and Sudarshan – are brought in a grand procession to the bathing platform for their ceremonial annual ablutions. Along with recitation of the mantras from the *Vedas*, 108 pots of consecrated water is poured upon the deities. Then the deities are attired ceremonially in *'GajaVisha'*, before they retire into seclusion for fifteen days called *'Anavasara* period'. It is an occasion of great rejoicing and merry-making.

Vata Savitri

The fast of Vata Savitri is observed generally on the 13th day of the dark fortnight of Jyaishtha, but at some places it is also observed on Jyaishtha Purnima. It is meant only for the married women. The Hindu married women observe this fast for the sake of longevity and well being of their husbands.

The story of Savitri and Satyavan is well known. According to the scriptures, Savitri, the daughter of King Aswapati, was the lover of Satyavan, whom she married, though she was warned by a seer that Satyavan had only one year to live. On the fateful day, Satyavan went out to cut wood, and Savitri followed him like his shadow. As fate would have it, Satyavan fell down and died and as she supported him, she saw a figure, who told her that he was Yama, the god of death and had come to take away the soul of Satyavan. Yama carried off his soul towards his abode, the Yamlok, but Savitri followed him. Her devotion so pleased Yama that he had to finally restore her husband's life. Like Savitri, it is the desire of every Hindu woman never to live and die as a widow.

CELEBRATIONS

Vata is a sacred tree among the Hindus. When Satyavan died, Savitri had worshipped the *Vata* (banyan tree). So, on Vata Savitri day, women get up early in the morning and having bathed they go to worship *Vata* in groups wearing gay raiments. They ceremonially water the tree, sprinkle *Kumkum* (red powder) on it, wrap raw cotton threads round its trunk, and then they go round it seven times which is called the *parikrama*.

On returning home they paint a *Vata* on a sanctified wall with turmeric powder and sandal and worship it. After breaking the fast, fruits, clothes and such other articles are given in charity in a bamboo basket to the Brahmins. They tell the story of Satyavan-Savitri among themselves and pray for the prosperity and good health of their respective husbands.

Anant Chaturdashi

It falls on the 14th day of the bright fortnight of Bhadra (August-September). On this auspicious day Vishnu sleeping on the bed of Anant (the Serpent Shesh) in the milky ocean is worshipped and meditated upon. While Vishnu slumbers on Anant, his consort Lakshmi massages his feet.

CELEBRATIONS

On this day fast is observed and fruits, sweets, flowers, etc. are offered to Vishnu in worship. A raw thread coloured in turmeric paste and having 14 knots is also tied on the upper right arms while meditating on Shesh-shayya Vishnu. This ensures protection against evil, and brings prosperity and happiness. The Pandav princes in exile were advised by Sri Krishna to observe this fast to regain their lost kingdom, wealth reputation and happiness.

Ganesh Chaturthi

Ganesh or Vinayak Chaturthi is one of the most popular Hindu festivals celebrated all over India as the birthday of Lord Ganesh, the elephant-headed god. It falls on the fourth day of the bright half of Bhaadra (August-September).

SIGNIFICANCE

Ganesh is the god of wisdom, learning, prudence, success and power. He is invoked or propitiated at the beginning of every activity. Being the *Vighnesha* or the remover of the obstacles, he is propitiated at the start of every activity, whether it is a journey, marriage, initiation, house construction, the writing of a book or even writing a letter.

He is a great scribe and a scholar of the religious lore and scriptures. Ganesh acted as the scribe and wrote down the *Mahabharata* as dictated by the seer Vyas. He is also the lord of *Ganas*, the hosts of Shiva. He bears a single tusk (Ekdanta) and holds in his four hands a shell, a discus, a goad and a lotus and is always accompanied by his mount, the rat. Ganesh is a great lover of sweets and fruits. He is also the presiding deity of *Muladhara Chakra* (plexus) or the psychic centre in the human body where the *Kundalini Shakti* resides.

HISTORY

There are two very interesting myths about his birth and how he came to possess the head of an elephant. One myth relates that disliking Lord Shiva's surprise visits during her baths, Parvati formed a human figure out of her scurf into a man's figure and gave it life. Then, she placed this person, later called Ganesh, to guard her bath-house entrance. Shiva came and tried to enter but when Ganesh barred his way, he cut off his head. It greatly angered Parvati, and so ultimately Shiva had to send someone to fetch another head for Ganesh. The first creature found was an elephant. Its head was brought and planted on Ganesh's shoulders.

Another version says that Parvati was blessed with a beautiful son. All the gods assembled to see and admire the son of Shiva-Parvati except Shani. Shani desisted from it because he was under the curse that whomsoever he beheld will be burnt to ashes. But Parvati insisted that Shani should also see and admire her son. As soon as he had a glimpse of Ganesh, Ganesh's head was burnt to ashes. Parvati cursed Shani for having killed her son, but Brahma intervened and consoled her by saying that if the first available head was planted on her son's shoulders, he would be alive again. So Vishnu set forth on his Garuda in search of it and the first creature he found was an elephant sleeping beside a river. He cut off its head and it was fixed on Ganesh's body.

Similarly there are numerous interesting legendary stories accounting for Ganesh's birth and his having only one tusk.

HOW TO CELEBRATE THE GANESH FESTIVAL

A life-like clay model of Lord Ganesh is made 2-3 months prior to the day of Ganesh Chaturthi. The size of this idol may vary from 3/4th of an inch to over 25 feet.

On the day of the festival, it is placed on raised platforms in homes or in elaborately decorated outdoor tents for people to view and pay their homage. The priest, usually clad in red silk *dhoti* and shawl, then invokes life into the idol amidst the chanting of *mantras*. This ritual is the *pranapratishhtha*. After this the *shhodashopachara* (16 ways of paying tribute) follows. Coconut, jaggery, 21 *modakas* (rice flour preparation), 21 *durva* (trefoil) blades and red flowers are offered. The idol is anointed with red unguent *(rakta chandan)*. Throughout the ceremony, *Vedic* hymns from the *Rig Veda* and *Ganapati Atharva Shirsha Upanishad*, and *Ganesha stotra* from the *Narada Purana* are chanted.

For 10 days, from *Bhadrapad Shudh Chaturthi* to the *Ananta Chaturdashi*, Ganesh is worshipped. On the 11th day, the image is taken through the streets in a procession accompanied with dancing, singing, to be immersed in a river or the sea symbolizing a ritual see-off of the Lord in his journey towards his abode in Kailash while taking away with him the misfortunes of all men and women. All join in this final procession shouting "*Ganapathi Bappa Morya, Purchya Varshi Laukariya*" (O father Ganesh, come again early next year). After the final offering of coconuts, flowers and camphor are made, people carry the idol to the river to immerse it.

The whole community comes to worship Ganesh in beautifully done tents. These also serve as the venue for free medical checkup, blood donation camps, charity for the poor, drama performances, films, devotional songs, etc. during the days of the festival.

Haritalika Teej

Haritalika fast (vow) is observed on the 3rd day of the bright half of Bhaadra (August-September). This fast is observed by the Hindu women in honour of Goddess Parvati and her consort Shiva, and their idols are worshipped ceremonially.

HISTORY AND SIGNIFICANCE

Parvati, the daughter of Himalaya and Maina, desirous of having Shankar as her husband, underwent severe *tapas* and finally had him as her lord and husband.

CELEBRATIONS

On this day married women worship the divine couple, and observe strict fast to ensure conjugal happiness and prosperity. Unmarried girls do so to have suitable husbands of their choice. Brahmins are given money and other things in charity, unmarried girls are fed and the aspirant women tell the story of Haritalika among themselves and break the fast in the evening. The next morning they worship the sun by offering water.

Janmashthami

Janmashthami marks the celebration of the birth of Lord Krishna. On the eighth day of the black half of Bhaadra (August) Sri Krishna, the eighth *Avtar* or incarnation of Vishnu was born. Therefore, this day is known as Janmashthami or Krishna-Janmashthami.

SIGNIFICANCE

This auspicious day of the birth of Krishna, the direct manifestation of Vishnu, is celebrated in all parts of India with eclat and great enthusiasm. In the *Bhagvad gita*, Krishna declares, "All this universe has been created by me, all things exist in me". Arjuna addresses him as "the supreme universal spirit, the supreme dwelling, the eternal person, divine, prior to the gods, unborn, omnipresent". His life is described in great detail in the *Purans* like *Harivamsha* and *Shrimad Bhagvatam*. The circumstances in which he was born were quite peculiar and mysterious. He incarnated himself primarily to destroy evil and wickedness and to establish *Dharma*.

HISTORY

The demon king Kansa was a great and dreaded tyrant, but he loved his sister Devaki, and at her marriage with Vasudev, out of great affection, he drove their marriage chariot. Then, all of a sudden everything went topsy-turvy when an oracle told him that the eighth child of Devaki shall be the cause of his doom and death. At this he would have killed her then and there, but Vasudev intervened and promised to give him over each and every child born to them. They kept their promise, and Kansa killed the six children born to them one after the other. The couple could do nothing except remain mute witness to this act of cruelty, for they were chained inside the prison and kept under strict vigil. The seventh child born to them was saved by divine grace.

The eighth son, Krishna, when he was born, it so happened that with divine grace, the guards fell asleep, their chains loosened and the gates of the prison cell opened.

Vasudev took the child Krishna to his friend Nand's house in Gokul. He entrusted his son with Nand and in exchange carried back the baby girl born to Nand and Yashoda. When Kansa heard of the birth of a girl child, he at once rushed to the prison cell, and lifted the female child high, catching it by the feet. When he was about to dash her against a wall she slipped from Kansa's grip and assuming the beautiful form of the Divine Mother vanished in the sky saying, "Wretch! thy destroyer is flourishing in Gokul". People at Gokul were rejoiced at the birth of a son to Nand and Yashoda. Yashoda was quite unaware of the exchange that had taken place during the night. Krishna grew up in Gokul and later killed Kansa.

CELEBRATIONS

The Janmashthami celebrations start right from the early morning with a bath in sacred waters and prayers. The celebration reaches its climax at midnight with the rising of the moon which marks the divine birth. On this auspicious day strict fast is observed which is broken only after the timing of the birth of Lord Krishna at midnight. Plenty of sweets are made like *laddoos/laddige, chakli, kheer,* etc. The temples and homes are decorated, scenes depicting Krishna's birth and his childhood pranks etc. are staged with models, both live and inanimate. Child Krishna's image is placed in a richly decorated swing and rocked with tender care all the day by the devotees. At midnight time after the birth of Lord Krishna, a small image of toddling Krishna is bathed in *Charnamrit,* amidst chanting of hymns, blaring of the conches, ringing of the bells and joyous shouting of 'victory to Krishna'.

In Brij Mandal, especially in Gokul, Mathura (Uttar Pradesh), Udipi (Karnataka) and Guruvayoor (Kerala), this festival is celebrated with great religious fervour and enthusiasm and the special deliberations of the day are relayed on the T.V. People from distant places congregate at Mathura and Vrindavan on this day to participate in the festival. The piety and fast observed on this day ensures the birth of good sons, and salvation after death. Reading and recitation of the *Bhagvatam* and *Geet Govidam* are recommended on this day.

Nag Panchami

Nag Panchami is observed on the 5th day of the bright half of Shraavan (July-August). Kaliya was a deadly serpent that inhabited the River Yamuna. Its venom was so vile that it poisoned the river and killed the crops and animals in the region. Sri Krishna killed Kaliya and liberated the people. Naag Panchami has been celebrated ever since in the region.

Symbolically, the snake god is always seen in a positive sense as an ornament around the neck of Shiv. So the festival also has mythological importance. The legend behind it goes like this: Once upon a time a farmer accidentally killed the young ones of a snake family while tilling his farm, thus inviting the wrath of the mother snake. In a fit of anger and craving for revenge, she bit the farmer's family in the night. Her deadly poison turned their blood blue.

She then left to bite the eldest married daughter who had painted images of snakes with sandalwood paste and was worshipping them in great faith by offering milk. The rage of the snake mother subsided and she blessed the woman. She returned to the farmer's family and sucked her venom out of their bodies. Ever since, the worship of the snake god has become common. Nag panchmi has special importance for the horoscopes having *Kaal Sarpa Yoga*. *Kaal Sarpa Yoga* is an important *yoga* found in horoscopes, which is formed when all the seven planets are hemmed in between the nodes i.e. Rahu and Ketu. However Rahu should come near the ascendant and Ketu should be away from it. When the situation is reverse, it is called *Kalamrit Yoga* and not *Kaal Sarpa Yoga*.

Rahu is the dragon's head and Ketu is the dragons tail. When the planets are hemmed between them, it will appear as though a snake *(Kaal)* is ready to devour all of them. That is why it is called *Kaal Sarpa Yoga*.

PROCESSION

In the rural areas, the setting sun is a witness to processions of gaily-decorated bullock carts, moving to nearby Shiva temples. Once there, excitement and merry-making take over, going well into the night. The men also set free the snakes they had captured the week before.

CELEBRATIONS

On this day, cobras and snakes are worshipped with offering of milk, sweets, flowers, and even sacrifices. The images of Nag deities made of silver, stone, wood (or painted on the wall) are first bathed with water and milk, and then worshipped with the reciting of the following *mantras*:

Nagah breeta dhavantih shantimapnoti vai vibhoh,
Sashanti lok ma sadhya modate shashttih samah.

Snakes and cobras are held in awe and reverence in India. They are worshipped and offered prayers on the Nag Panchami day. Fast is observed and Brahmins are fed on this day. The piety observed on this day is considered a sure protection against the fear of snake-bite. At many places real cobras and snakes are worshipped and fairs held.

As part of the traditions of the festival, women draw figures of snakes on the walls of their houses using a mixture of black powder, cow dung and milk. Then offerings of milk, *ghee*, water and rice are made to the snake god.

SIGNIFICANCE

On this day digging the earth is prohibited, as the serpents live under the earth or in the nether world and digging may hurt or annoy them. The various *Purans* like *Agni Puran, Skanda Puran, Narad Puran,* etc. give details of snake-worship and its significance.

The Nags, as mythical creatures, are semi-divine beings. They are said to have sprung from Kadru, the wife of Rishi Kashyapa, and inhabit *Patal* or the regions below the earth, where they reign in great splendour. They roam around the land wearing lustrous jewels and ornaments. The thousand-hooded Shesh Naag or Anant is the most powerful of them and revered even by the gods. He bears the whole earth on his crown. When he nods or yawns, the earth, with its oceans and mountains, begins to tremble.

Nag Panchami is also observed as Bhratri Panchami, and women having brothers worship snakes, and keep fast to propitiate Nags so that their beloved brothers do not fall victim to snakebite. The genealogy of serpents in India has been given a semi-human attribute. Some of them intermarried with men, as Ulupi married Arjuna. The snake deities are also regarded as the custodians of the treasures of land and sea.

Onam

Onam is the most famous festival of Kerala. It is celebrated in the Malayalam month of Chingam, corresponding to Bhaadra (August-September). It is a harvest festival characterized by four days of feasting, merry-making and the famous 'snake' boat races. These boats may be paddled by up to 100 persons. The snake boat race of Alleppey, held annually in August, is the most prominent of all. The number of the paddlers rowing a boat indicates the affluence of the man whom it belongs to.

PROCESSION

A clay moulded image of Vamana, the fifth incarnation of Vishnu, is worshipped on this day in the temples and the houses.

HISTORY

On the second day of the festival, it is believed that Bali, the legendary king of Kerala, visits his kingdom and people. The *Purans* relate a very interesting story about Vamana and Bali.

Bali was a virtuous demon king. He was son of Virochana and grandson of Prahlad. He did great *tapasya* and defeated Indra and extended his rule and authority over the three worlds. The harassed and humiliated gods prayed Vishnu for protection, and he incarnated himself as Vamana, the son of Aditi and Kashyapa. Relying on Bali's reputation for charity, Vamana approached him and begged from him the gift of three paces of land for making a sacrificial altar. As soon as this request was accepted, Vamana turned giant-like and by taking the first two paces he measured all the earth and the heaven, and thus won back the whole of Bali's kingdom for the gods. But then being reminded of Bali's merits, generosity and other qualities, he stopped short, and left to Bali the nether regions or the *Patal Lok*. Bali is also called Mahabali, and his capital was Mahabalipuram, near Madras.

CELEBRATIONS

Bali was also permitted by Vamana to visit his lost kingdom and the subjects once a year, and this visit is regularly celebrated in Kerala, and particularly in Malabar by his devotees on the day of Onam. To welcome their ancient good king Bali, the people of Kerala tidy up their houses and environs, decorate the houses with flowers and mango leaves and also arrange grand feasts and many types of amusements. The spectacular snake-boat race marks the crowning glory of these amusements and games. A clay cone symbol of Bali is placed in front of houses, decorated with sandalwood paste and vermilion and colourful *rangoli* designs are drawn in the yard. The elders give the gifts of clothes and other things to youngsters.

There is no deity associated with Onam and there is no special Puja, still the housewife performs daily rituals with a little extra piety.

The celebrations are crowned by a grand feast known as *Ona Sadya*. The cuisine is elaborate with several vegetables. Food is served on banana leaves, and special dishes are served like *pachadi*, *kitchadi*, *Kaalan*, *Olan*, *Parippu*, *Thoran*, *Ghee*, *Sambar*, *Pappad*, *Banana Chips*, *Pickle*, etc. Milk pudding called *Paalpayasam* is the special dish for Onam.

Putrada Ekadashi

*P*utra ekadashi is observed on the 11th day of the bright half of Shravan. As the name itself shows, it is observed particularly by parents wishing to get a son. The observance of fast and piety on this day is said to result in getting a son, and it also destroys the sins of the aspirants. Like other Ekadashis, it is also dedicated to Lord Vishnu.

Fast is observed, Vishnu is worshipped and meditated upon, and the Brahmins, learned in the *Vedas* and sacred religious lore, are given food, robes, money, etc., in charity on this day. At night the aspirants should sleep in the room where Vishnu has been worshipped.

HISTORY AND SIGNIFICANCE

A legend supports this belief. In ancient days there was a king called Mahijit who ruled the earth from his capital Mohishmati. He was very wise, rich, religious, powerful and peace-loving, but he had no issues. This used to worry him day and night. One day he called an assembly of the learned, wise and intellectual people, seers and *rishis* and put before them his problem.

In the assembly there was one Rishi Lomesh, most learned and holy and the possessor of the knowledge of *Brahman*. He told the King that in the previous birth he had prevented a cow from drinking from a pond on the Ekadashi falling on the bright fortnight of Shravan, and thereby he had incurred a curse of remaining issueless in this life. He advised the king to propitiate the gods and atone for his sins by observing fast and piety on this day, by keeping a night vigil and spending his time in meditation, chanting the praises of Lord Hari. The king and the queen did accordingly. They observed a strict fast, gave jewels, money, robes, elephants, horses and cows to the Brahmins in charity; meditated upon Vishnu and kept a night vigil. Consequently after 12 months they were blessed with a handsome son, heir to the throne.

Similarly the Ekadashi falling in the dark half of the Shravan should be observed. This Ekadashi is known as Kamada Ekadashi, or the wish-fulfilling Ekadashi.

PUTRADA EKADASHI   113

Raksha Bandhan

The festival of Raksha Bandhan is observed on the full moon day of Shravan (July-August). The word '*Raksha*' means protection. On this auspicious day women and girls tie an amulet-like thread round the right hand wrists of their brothers as a token of protection against evil during the ensuing year.

HISTORY

According to Hindu scriptures Shachi, the consort of Indra, the god of heaven, tied such a *mantra* charged thread round the right wrist of her husband when he was disgraced in the battle by the demon forces. Indra again fought and gained a convincing victory over the demons, and recovered his lost capital Amaravati. The sacred amulet helped him in defeating the enemy.

SIGNIFICANCE

The thread is called '*Rakhi*' and is made of a few colourful cotton or silk twisted threads or threads of gold or silver. The brothers give their sisters gifts of money, clothes and other valuable things in return. Sisters feed their brothers with sweets, dry fruits and other delicacies on this occasion.

CELEBRATIONS

Priests and Brahmins also tie this kind of thread round the wrists of the right hands of their patrons and receive gifts. They recite a *mantra* or a sacred hymn while doing so to charge the thread with the power of protection.

Yen baddho Bali Raja Danavendro Mahabalah,
Ten tvam Pratibandhanami rakshe ma chal ma chal.

The thread charged with the power of the *mantra* protects the wearer from every possible evils. Coconut *Barfi* is prepared specially on this day.

In South India, it is celebrated as Avani Avittam. The holy thread *(Upanayan)* is changed and libation of water is offered to the ancestors and *Rishis* on this occasion. The new thread is worshipped with saffron and turmeric paste before wearing and the old one is discarded in the water of a pond, a tank or a river. This day is especially significant for a Brahmin boy who has recently been invested with an *upanayan* (holy thread). It reminds him of the glory and significance of religion. *Vedas* are also read and recited on this day.

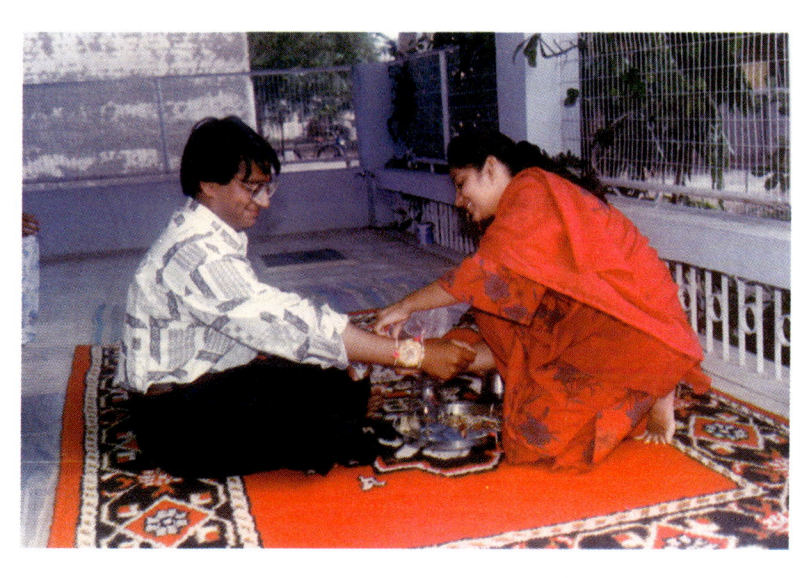

In Bombay coconuts are offered to the sea-god Varuna on this occasion. Exchange of sweets, setting up of fairs, visiting the relatives and friends, sending the 'rakhis' by post to brothers living at far off places, and remembering the *Rishis* and *Gurus*, whom we are indebted to, for their guidance and spiritual knowledge are other highlights of this festival.

Shravani Mela

In the sacred month of Shravan, a grand fair is held in Bihar at Deoghar. During this month devotees fill up water from the holy Ganga at Sultanganj and carry it on their shoulders to Deoghar and offer it on Shiva Lingam. The 100 kms distance from Sultanganj to Deoghar is covered by trekking. All along the long route the pilgrims go on chanting *"Bol Bam! Bol Bam!"* Thousands of them, all clad in saffron, carry the sacred water in *kanwars,* and continue trekking day and night, in rain or scorching sun to their destination. In the shrine at Deoghar pilgrims throng in large numbers carrying *Gangajal* and shouting. *"Bol Bam!"* They present a unique and unforgettable sight.

Teej

Teej, purely a festival of girls and ladies, is sacred to Goddess Parvati, the consort of Lord Shiva. It was on this auspicious day that Parvati was reunited with Shiva after a long separation. She declared this day sacred and auspicious and said that whosoever invoked her on this day would possess whatever they desired. It is celebrated annually in most parts of India, and especially in the state of Rajasthan.

SIGNIFICANCE

Festivals are the very essence of life for the people of Rajasthan. Peacocks dance in ecstasy, women rejoice by swinging on rope swings in gardens and lilting melodies heralding the festival of Teej echo all round. The festival of Teej reflects the magic of the monsoon. Teej is celebrated on the third day of the waxing moon in the month of Shravan (July-August).

PROCESSION

People pray for a cool shower at the time of the procession. Gorgeous processions bearing images of Parvati are taken out escorted by caparisoned elephants, camels and horses, which symbolize bride Parvati leaving her parents' home for her husband. Before the procession starts the goddess is ceremonially worshipped and prayed.

CELEBRATIONS

Swings are hung on the trees and in the houses, where the maidens and women amuse themselves by swinging. They wear gorgeous apparels in red, green and gold, and paint delicate designs on their hands and feet with *henna*, and sing songs in praise of the goddess and the monsoon. Thus, it also welcomes the monsoon. Fairs are held on this occasion and people enjoy themselves to their full.

Teej is essentially a women's festival. Women dress up in their finery to worship the goddess. Girls engaged to be married receive gifts from their future in-laws a day before the festival: the gift called *Sindhara* consists of *lac* bangles, a special dark *henna laheria* and a sweet called *ghewar*.

Tirupati Festival

In the month of Bhaadra (August-September), a grand festival is held annually at Tirupati, the seat of Lord Venkateshwara, and a manifestation of Lord Vishnu. This festival lasts for 10 days, and during this festival devotees from all over the country congregate here to seek Lord Venkateshwara's blessing to attain material and spiritual gains. Even on ordinary days over 20,000 pilgrims, on an average, visit the shrine to pray and worship the deity. People usually make a pilgrimage to this shrine once they overcome some difficulties or after wish fulfilment. Mammoth crowds queue up for hours every day to have a *darshan* of the deity.

This is one of the richest temples in the world. It is situated on Tirumala hills – seven in number – which correspond to the seven hoods of the snake-god Adishesh, who forms the bed of Vishnu in the cosmic ocean. And because of these seven picturesque hills Venkateshwara is also known as the "Lord of the Seven Hills". Various *Purans* describe how and why this is an essential pilgrimage centre for each and every devout Hindu. It is a tradition here that devotees, whether men or women, shave their hair off as a votive offering for a wish fulfilled. Parents bring their very young children and perform their first tonsure at the lotus feet of the Lord.

Tulsidas Jayanti

Tulsidas Jayanti is celebrated on the seventh day of the bright half of Shravan. The great saint-poet Tulsidas was a contemporary of Akbar, the Great. He was born to Brahmin parents, but soon became an orphan, and was brought up and educated by a saint named Naraharidas. Naraharidas was instructed to do so by God in a dream. It is he who gave him the *mantra* of 'Ram-nam'. Tulsidas married and started living the life of a householder, but some chance words of his wife awakened in him his ardent *Bhakti* towards God, and he became a *sanyasi* and began to live in Varanasi.

There he wrote his well-known "*Ramacharit Manas*" besides a dozen other books. He wrote this masterpiece in the language of the common people for their benefit.

In the words of Grierson, "Over whole of the Gangetic region his work is better known than the *Bible* is in England". His *Ramayana* is verily the life-breath of the devout Hindus.

In no uncertain terms he has emphasized the significance of the path of devotion or *Bhakti* as a means of spiritual evolution and final liberation. He lays stress on the constant repetition of *Ram-nam*, because in this present era (*Kalikal*) knowledge, *yoga*, *samadhi* and dispassion are of little avail. Therefore, one must constantly recite the name of Rama with unwavering faith. The repetition of this name is greater than austerity, pilgrimage, oblation, discipline and fasts.

His own saintly example and the magic of his writings have done more for the spiritual upliftment of the masses than the teachings of hundreds of *gurus*. He and his works are so greatly revered that tradition regards him as Valmiki reborn. It is believed that he died on the same date, and a couplet is often quoted in this connection:

Samvat solah so assi, assi Gang ke tir,
Shravan shukla saptami Tulsi tajyo sharir.

CELEBRATIONS

On the auspicious day of his *Jayanti* and *Moksha*, fast is observed and charities are done. *Ramayana* is read and recited, Brahmins are fed, and Lord Rama, along with his consort Sita and devotee Hanuman, is worshipped with great religious fervour. In literary and social circles, discussions, lectures, seminars and symposiums on his teaching, life and works are organized.

Bhaiya Duj

Bhaiya Duj, symbolizing the deep affection between brothers and sisters, is celebrated on the second day of the bright fortnight of Kartik, which falls on the day next to Govardhan Puja. The married women invite their dear brothers to their respective homes, apply turmeric or sandalwood *tilaks* on their foreheads, tie a coloured thread (*moli*) around their right wrists, pray for their prosperity and longevity and then feast them on sweets and other delicacies. In return they receive valuable gifts. Unmarried girls do so at their parents' home.

Bhaiya Duj is also called the Yama Dvitiya, because this day also symbolizes the deep affection between Yama and his sister Yami. Sisters pray Yama for their brothers' longevity, good health and happiness, and observe strict fast. The Sun-born Yamuna, sister of Yama, is also worshipped on this day.

Chhath Puja
Festival of the Sun God

Chhath Puja is an Indian thanksgiving festival dedicated to the Sun god. During the celebrations of Chhath Puja, people gather on the banks of the River Ganges to bathe in its sacred water, pray and make ritual offerings to the Sun god. Chhath Puja is a highly elaborate festival noted for its impressive display of colourful costumes, music, singing and extravagant rituals.

A week after the festival of lights, Diwali, is the Chhath festival. For one full night and day, the people of Bihar literally live on the banks of the river Ganga when a ritual offering is made to the Sun god.

The word *Chhath* denotes the number six and thus the name itself serves as a reminder of this auspicious day on the festival almanac. The venue for this unique festivity is the river bank and since the river Ganga traverses the countryside of Bihar like a lifeline it is but appropriate that the rising and setting sun as witnessed on the banks of this river should be the ideal prayer propitiation locale.

With no temples to visit, or house to spruce up before the festival, one would conclude that Chhath Puja or prayer ritual would be an easy sail through. But that proves misplaced euphemisms for, the ritual observances of this occasion would make a medieval Franciscan Order appear frivolous.

Adult married women of the household become shining examples of what they set out to preach. There is complete abstinence from performing household chores, as younger women and even children are encouraged to take over these mundane tasks. Thus shielded from profanities, they begin a thorough spring cleaning of the kitchen fire and the pans that would be used to prepare the *prasad* or food offerings to the Sun god. The usual kitchen *chulha* with the telltale marks of spilt over food are removed by a meticulous application of liquid cow dung and clay. The frying pan, cooking wok, and the ladles are purified with a brisk cleaning with coconut husk and ash till they shine as silver.

It is the bounty of the harvest which is deemed a fit offering for the solar deity. Newly pounded rice is soaked and made into a paste. Dry fruits, nuts and slivers of coconut are used as garnish and the cooked lump is then rolled in the palms, into hardened *laddoos*. Wheat flour becomes the main ingredient for the traditional cake locally termed as *thekuwa*.

Then on the eve of the sixth day, the excitement mounts to a solemn crescendo. Instead of the usual laughter accompanying the previous Deepawali festival, this time it is sacrilegious to crack a joke or even make a chance remark as the processional walk to the riverside leaves the doorstep. Children are warned of dire consequences, then and there, in case any one of them has the slightest inclination. A high-pitched sing-song of hymnal sounds marks the start of this journey and, what began as a trickle from the doorstep, becomes a surging crowd of devotees as one nears the river banks. No one tells the hour of prayer or performance but, magically, the procession is timed to an accuracy that would be the envy of a drill sergeant.

The men in the procession are bare-chested and seem not to feel the nip in the chilly November air, which gets more marked as the breeze becomes cooler near the approaching waters. The lead figure for every group carries a basket of bamboo weaves. It is held high above the crowd's hands for fear of it being profaned by the chance touch of a passing stranger and thus an unworthy offering to the mighty giver of light. Within it are the *laddoos*, the *kuwas* and of course the fruits of the season. The coconut, in its surround of coir and shell, a bunch of bananas, an orange or two and always an earthen lamp, smothered in cotton cloth, dyed in turmeric, are the unchangeable contents.

At the riverbank, the fading light of the evening sun makes one mind one's step. No one can afford to let slip or falter as that would mean an evil portent but since the shallow bank stretches endlessly, they're really in no reason to push or jostle. The low-lying edge of the waters is slippery as the soil is alluvial but the rows of country boats, all geared to take passengers and offerings mid-stream in comparative safety, make the task easier. Then, as the western sky of early winter turns rosy, the scene is a concerted vision of devotion as countless upstretched arms hold aloft the glistening bamboo trays and baskets. The veiled oil lamps are gently glowing and a chorus of hymns rings the air. The minutes pass, a gloom descends and the faces become blurred as the crowds walk back along the narrow path, leading away from the river front.

Having paid homage to the setting sun, the next day, one must make ready for the daybreak obeisance. This is the crucial part of the ritual and the journey towards the river begins when not even the slightest hint of sunlight is visible. It is a mahogany dark sky outside as the festival falls during the dark phase of the moon. One can tell when the riverbank is near from the smell of dew-soaked grass and the inky waters can only be decoded by the sound of a soft lapping. This time the faces turn eastwards and instead of just standing on the riverbank, they enter the water for the customary holy dip. In the meantime, the precious baskets are left securely under a temporary canopy, made of freshly harvested sugar cane stalks. The four-sided platform is specially made with its corners decorated with terracotta lamps shaped like elephants or birds.

The accompaniments of sandalwood paste, vermilion, wet rice, flowers and fruits, covered with red dyed cotton cloth, to ward off evil designs and spirits, add the right note of sanctity. The priests in the medley of worshippers readily oblige devotees with chantings and prayers as the families stand around their altar with folded hands, closed eyes and devoted hearts to offer their prayers to the giver of all life in the world. Once the first streaks of light appear on the horizon, men and women, dressed in their *saris* and *dhotis* (loin-cloth) plunge into the shallow waters. Having found a foothold and completely oblivious of the chilling waters, they begin the timeless *mantra* of the *Rig Veda*, specific to the Sun–the *Gayatri Mantra*.

It is this unquestioned faith, a reminder about the basics of human existence, a conscious upkeep of the environment in its benevolence and bounty that becomes integral to the currency of living and believing.

PLACE OF CHHATH PUJA CELEBRATIONS

Chhath Puja is celebrated mainly in the northern regions of the Indian state of Bihar. The festival takes place on the banks of the River Ganges, in homes and at the Sun temple of Baragaon, two kilometers outside Nalanda, in Bihar. Chhath Puja is also celebrated in Varanasi in the state of Uttar Pradesh.

Deepawali

Deepawali or the Festival of Lights is an important and most popular festival celebrated throughout the country in one form or the other. It falls on the last day of the dark half of Kartik (October-November). As a matter of fact, it is a five-day long festival, but the main celebrations take place on the day of Deepawali.

Deepawali, which leads us into truth and light, is celebrated on a nation-wide scale on Amavasya – the 15th day of the dark fortnight of the Hindu month of Ashwin (October / November) every year. It symbolises that age-old culture of our country which teaches us to vanquish ignorance that subdues humanity and to drive away darkness that engulfs the light of knowledge. Deepawali, even today in this modern world projects the rich and glorious past of our country and teaches us to uphold the true values of life.

The Sanskrit word "Deepawali" Deepa meaning light and *Avali* meaning a row, means a row of lights and indeed illumination forms its main attraction. Every home – lowly or mightly – the hut of the poor or the mansion of the rich – is alight with the orange glow of twinkling *diyas*-small earthen lamps – to welcome Lakshmi, goddess of wealth and prosperity. Multi-coloured *Rangoli* designs, floral decorations and fireworks lend grace and grandeur to this festival which heralds joy, mirth and happiness in the ensuing year

This festival is celebrated on a grand scale in almost all the regions of India and is looked upon mainly as the beginning of new year. As such the blessings of Lakshmi, the celestial consort of Lord Vishnu are invoked with prayers. Even countries like Guyana, Thailand, Trinidad and Malaysia celebrate this festival but in their own ways.

HISTORY

Deepawali is associated with several legends. One myth says that on this auspicious day Lakshmi, the goddess of wealth and good fortune roams about and visits the houses of people. Therefore, people tidy up their homes, establishments and shops and decorate them lavishly to welcome the goddess. In the night she is worshipped with great devotion. It also commemorates the triumph of Lord Rama over Ravana, and Rama's return to Ayodhya. It is also on this day that Krishna killed the demon Narkasura.

CELEBRATIONS

A few days before the festival, the houses are completely cleaned and painted. The courtyards, the gates and the places of worship are decorated with *bandanvars*, flowers, intricate coloured paperwork and at night every nook and corner of the house is illuminated with earthen lamps or candles, and fireworks are displayed till late midnight. On the day of Deepawali, people get up early in the morning, clean their home and after the completion of daily chores, attire themselves in their best clothes and move around freely in the atmosphere of gaiety, mirth, greetings and festivity. Lots of sweets are prepared and exchanged along with greetings.

On this occasion people ask for each other's forgiveness for the wrongs done knowingly or unknowingly and mutual relations are re-established and strengthened. Thus, all enmity is forgiven and forgotten and people embrace one another. At night, Lakshmi along with Ganesh is worshipped and in business, old accounts are closed and new ones are opened. People throng the *bazaars* and streets during the night in order to watch and appreciate the illumination. Special shops and *bazaars* are also set up on this occasion, and there is brisk buying of sweets, utensils, clothes, jewellery, toys, etc.

Deepawali also marks the advent of new season and the sowing of new crop-seeds. The new Vikrama Era begins on this day. The famous King Vikramaditya, after whom the era is named, was crowned on this day. In Bengal, Kali is worshipped with great fervour and devotion on this day. The Jains celebrate Deepawali as a day of final liberation and '*moksha*' of Lord Mahavira. Similarly Swami Dayanand Saraswati, the founder of the Arya Samaj, attained salvation on this day. The great Swami Rama Tirtha also entered his final *jal-samadhi* on this tithi. At great Jain shrines like that of Pavapuri in Bihar, and Girnar in Gujarat, special puja festivals are held, sacred scriptures read and recited and Lord Mahavira worshipped. Thus, this great festival of lights symbolizes man's urge to move towards light of truth from darkness of ignorance and unhappiness.

Devuthani Ekadashi

Vishnu slumbers for four months from the eleventh day of the bright half of Ashadh (June-July) till the tenth day of the bright half of Kartik (October-November). And, then, he gets up on the eleventh day, which is known as Devuthani Ekadashi. During these four months all other gods sleep and so auspicious ceremonies like marriage, thread ceremony, etc. are not performed.

CELEBRATIONS

On this day, ladies observe fast, worship Vishnu and sing hymns in praise of various gods and goddesses around a cowdung-cake fire. It also marks the beginning of eating the new agricultural produce of the season especially sugarcane and water chestnuts. It is an important rural festival, and is observed with much gaiety and festivity in the countryside. From this day onward, marriages etc. can be held as it marks the beginning of the auspicious time for ceremonies. It is believed that tired after killing the great demon Shankhasura, Vishnu went to sleep for a period of four months and the other deities followed suit.

Dhan Teras

Two days prior to Deepawali, on the 13th day of the dark half of Kartik, Dhan Teras or Dhanvantri Triyodashi is observed with great mirth and gaiety. Dhanvantri, the physician of gods, who appeared as one of the several precious entities at the churning of the ocean, is worshipped on this day, especially by the physician community. He is the father of the Indian medical science and Ayurveda is attributed to him. He is also called Sudha-pani, because he appeared from the ocean, carrying nectar in his hands.

People get up early at dawn, cleanse themselves, put on new attire and observe fast. In the evening an earthen lamp is invariably lit in front of every house, and the fast is broken. New utensils are bought on this day because it is regarded very auspicious.

Durga Puja
Navratra

Navratras are observed twice a year, one in the month of Chaitra, preceding Ramnavami, and then in Ashvin (September-October) preceding Dussehra. This nine-day Navratra commences with the new moon of Ashvin and terminates with Mahanavami, on the ninth lunar day of the bright half of the month. During these nine days, devotees keep strict fast and worship Durga. The style of observing Navratra in different parts of the country may be different, but its sole aim is to propitiate Mother Durga and to seek her blessings.

HISTORY

It is believed that in ancient times, a demon called Mahishasura earned the favour of Lord Brahma after long meditation and prayers. Shiva blessed him with a boon that no man or god would be able to kill him. Then Mahishasura started killing people mercilessly and even drove the gods out of heaven. The gods complained to Shiva, who opened his third eye with anger and concentrated the energy coming out of it to form a woman and thus Durga was born. Riding a lion, she attacked Mahishasura and beheaded him.

PROCESSION

On Pratipada (first lunar day of bright half of Ashvin) an earthen pitcher filled with water, its mouth covered with green leaves and an earthen lid, is installed with invocation of Ganesh, the god of learning and wisdom, and then Durga is invoked and ritually worshipped with *durva* grass, flowers, leaves, lamps, incense, new grains, raiments, etc. Barley seeds are also sprouted and grown in a pot on this occasion, and the same is worn in caps and on ears on the final day. Unmarried girls below the age of ten are also worshipped and given gifts during these nine days. A clarified butter lamp is always kept burning before the installed pitcher during the celebration, and daily *Durga-saptashti*, *Devi Bhagvat Puran* and *Devi Mahatmya* section of the *Markandeya Puran* are recited.

CELEBRATION

In Bengal, Durga Puja is celebrated with great excitement and festivity and huge *puja* pavilions or *pandals*, with an idol of the ten-armed Durga, set up at various places.

Durga, the beautiful but fierce goddess, is shown riding the lion and killing the demon Mahishasura. In each of her ten hands she holds one of the gods' special battle related items: Vishnu's discus, Shiva's trident, Varuna's conch shell, Agni's flaming dart, Vayu's bow, Surya's quiver, Indra'a thunderbolt, Kubera's club, a garland of snakes from Shesh, and as a charger, a lion from the Himalaya. A fierce battle raged between Durga and Mahishasura, but finally she killed him with the trident.

Durga Puja surpasses all other festivals in Bengal in its popularity and mass appeal. During the celebration, music, dance, drama and other entertainments are performed before the enthralled audience. The images of goddess Durga are taken on the final day in triumphal procession from all corners, coverging on the river where they are ceremonially immersed. Durga Puja is more than a ritual as it enriches the lives of people with a new enlightenment, and produces a feverish literary and artistic activity. It is believed that Durga visits her parents Himavan and Maina only during these days in a year. The final day marks the end of this brief visit when she leaves for Mount Kailash, the abode of her husband Lord Shiva. Ladies give an emotion-charged and affectionate sendoff to Durga, and the ceremony is characterized with a daughter's departure to her husband's house.

POPULARITY

Durga Puja is the most important festival in India. Durga Puja is more than a festival, it is a celebration of life, culture, popular customs and traditions. It is a time of reunion and rejuvenation to love, to share and to care. This festival provides a perfect platform to every Indian with rich cultural ethos and values to organize themselves under one roof.

Durga Puja is an important Hindu festival celebrated all over India with different rituals and festivities. It is celebrated in the month of September/October. The excited festivity is omnipresent during Durga Puja throughout India, specifically in the eastern part of India, particularly in West Bengal. The beautiful but fierce goddess on her lion is worshipped with great enthusiasm.

LEGENDS

Durga is the goddess of divine power against all evils. The story goes that Mahishasura, the buffalo demon, through years of praying, received a boon from Lord Brahma that no power can kill him which means he is invincible. But on gaining this power, he started ravaging the whole world and killing people. And finally he wanted to uproot the gods too. All the gods and godesses, in dismay, combined their powers to create a beautiful maiden, and each placed his or her most potent weapon in one of her ten hands. With the help of such great powers in her hands, she killed Mahishasura.

Riding a lion, her return in each year in the month of Aswin (September-October) also commemorates Rama's invocation of the goddess Durga before he went into battle with Ravana. The traditional image of the Bengali Durga follows the iconographic injunctions of the *Shastras*. It is similar to the Durga of Aihole and of Mahabalipuram (seventh century). The tableau of Durga with Kartik, Ganesh, Saraswati and Lakshmi, representing respectively the Protector, the Initiator of the *puja*, Knowledge and the Provider signifies the complete manifestation of the goddess.

Another legend has it that Lord

Rama went to rescue his abducted wife Sita from the grip of Ravana, the king of the demons in Lanka. Before starting for his battle with Ravana, Rama wanted the blessings of Devi Durga. Pleased with Rama's devotion, Durga appeared before him and blessed him. The battle started on the *saptami* and Ravana was finally killed on the *sandhikshan* i.e. the crossover period between *ashtami* and *navami* and was cremated on *dashami*. Since the period of this worship was different from the conventional festival time of spring or *basant*, this *puja* is also known as *akal-bodhan* or worship (*bodhan*) in an unconventional time (*a-kaal*).

One more view is that once the mother of Durga wished to see her daughter. Durga was permitted by Lord Shiva to visit her beloved mother only for nine days in a year. The festival of Durga Puja marks this visit and ends with the *Vijaya Dashami* day, when Goddess Durga leaves for her return to Mount Kailash.

RITUALS

Durga Puja is basically a festival with a series of rituals and *puja*. The making of Durga idols is also governed by rituals. The elemental ritual, which is most commonly followed, is that the ingredients that are used to make the idol of goddess Durga must come from the holy river Ganga. The idol of Durga is generally flanked by the idols of Lakshmi, Saraswati, Kartik and Ganesh. The image of Durga is positioned at the centre, and the background behind the whole group is called the *chaal-chitra*. The goddess sits atop a lion, which is her *vahan*. The favourite tableau is of her stabbing Mahishasura, the demon. It symbolizes the victory of goodness over evil. It is celebrated in different parts of India in different styles. But the basic aim is to propitiate *Shakti*, the Goddess in her aspect as power, to bestow upon man all wealth, auspiciousness, prosperity, knowledge, and all other potent powers.

Traditional and household Durga Puja festivities last for ten days. But the main ritual of Durga Puja spans a period of four days. *Debi-Paksha* is the name given to the fortnight from the new moon till the next full moon. This is the most propitious time for performing holy rites. The ritual of drawing the eyes on the image of the goddess is called *chakshu-daan*. Symbolising the process of infusing the image with the power of vision is done on the day of the new moon. The main *puja* starts from *Shasthi*, which is the sixth day after the new moon. On *Saptami*, the image of the goddess is infused with life. Early in the morning, the *pran* of the Devi is put inside the image after it is brought from a nearby river through the medium of a banana plant. The banana plant (*Kola Bou*) bathed and draped in a new yellow saree, resembles a newly-wed bride. *Ashtami* is universally accepted as the culminating point of the four-day celebrations. It was on this day that Durga had killed Mahishasura. The ritual of *Sandhipuja* marks *Sandhikkhan*, the juncture between *Ashtami* and *Nabami*. The main attraction of *Nabami* is the *Maha-Arati* held in the evening. On *Dashami*, the image is immersed in a river. *Bijoya* is a special ritual whereby peace and good relations are reaffirmed. Families exchange sweets and people embrace each other, vowing brotherhood. *Bijoya* continues till the next new moon, when *Kali Puja* is held.

FAIRS AND FESTIVITIES

Durga Puja has transcended geographical boundaries and reached every corner across the globe. The four-day fair has become an indispensable part of every one's life in India.

It is one of the biggest festivals in Bengal. Durga Puja is celebrated on a mass scale with *puja pandals* dotting nearly every corner of West Bengal. Community *pujas* in Bengal are organised in every locality. On the final day the idols are taken in elaborate processions to be immersed in the river or the pond. Such is the charm and seduction of the occasion that several big community *pujas* in the city are being sponsored by multi-national companies and commercial firms.

The inauguration starts on *Mahashasthi*. The main *puja* is for three days – *Mahasaptami*, *Mahaastami* and *Mahanavami*. Three days of *Mantras* and *Shlokas* and *Arati* and offerings – needs an expert priest to do this kind of Puja. Because of these facts, the number of *Pujas* held in the family has reduced and Durga Puja has mostly emerged as a community festival. The city of Calcutta takes a different look during these three days, especially at night. Millions of people come to the city and line up before the *pandals*. The streets are lighted and the electricians display different kind of light shows. The restaurants are packed and numerous temporary food stalls are opened thoughout the city.

Schools, colleges and offices remain closed during these four days. After the three days of *Puja*, on *Dashami*, the last day, a tearful farewell is offered to the goddess. The idols are carried in processions around the locality and finally are immersed in a nearby river or lake. People of Bengal all over the world celebrate this great event of their culture.

In West Bengal's neighbouring state Orissa, the festivals of Durga Puja is celebrated in a similar manner. Especially in the city of Cuttack a large number of idols of Durga and Mahadev are worshipped in profusely decorated *pandals*. Life comes to a standstill in the city as crowds pour into the Puja *pandals* to enjoy the festivities. On the day succeeding 'Vijaya Dasami', the last day of Dussehra, the images are taken in a spectacular procession for immersion in the river Kathajodi.

FOCUS ON BENGAL

History of Durga Puja in Bengal dates back to the Mughal era. According to historians, the first *Puja* was organised by Raja Kangshanarayan of Teherpur, Nadia and then Raja Jagatnarayan of Bhaduria followed soon after. Other Hindu kings too came forward and the *puja* spread far and wide to Gour, Raj Mahal, Murshidabad and Krishnagar.

By middle of 18th century, this festival had become the occasion for the nouveau riche *Babus* of Kolkata to flaunt their wealth. They invited Europeans every evening to grace the occasion. The British too participated enthusiastically and had *Prasad* and did *Pranam*, often lying prostrate on the ground. Some believe that the *Puja* of Suborno Chowdhury is the oldest in the city, started in 1610 near Behala Sakher Bazaar area. Second oldest is that of Govindaram Mitra of Kumartuli which started in the early 1800s. Next renowned is that Sovbazaar Raj Bar. But gradually collective enterprise replaced the individual initiative. It was in 1790, that 12 Brahmin friends in Guptipara, Hooghly, decided to institute community *Puja*. Subscriptions were raised from neighbours. Thus started Puja in Bengal which gained popularity by leaps and bounds. *Sarbojanin Durgotsab*, as we know it today, started off much later in Kolkata, in the 1920s, with Shimlaya Byayam Samiti and Bagbazar being the earliest. At present hundreds of *Pujas* are held in the city's lanes and bylanes. But Raja Ram Mohan Roy was the pioneer who promoted the idea of Durga Puja all over India, in pre-independence era. Yet over the years, the ritualistic aspect has been reduced to a large extent in the community *pujas*. The accent is clearly on crowd-pulling capacity. Earlier *Pandals* would be draped in the coloured cloth spread over tarpaulin held up by a bare framework of bamboo poles. Gradually it was the turn of the much brighter halogen lamps. Now of course, there are metal lamps. Innovative *pandals* take the cake in terms of generating visitors' volume.

Dussehra

Dussehra or Vijay Dashmi is a very popular Hindu festival, celebrated with eclat throughout the country. It is observed on the tenth day of the bright half of Ashwin (September-October).

CELEBRATIONS

It is a ten-day celebration, during which *'Ramlila'*, based on the epic story of *Ramayana*, is staged at various places in most of the cities and towns in northern India, with elaborate rituals. It presents a fine blending of music, dance, mime and poetry before an enthusiastic and religious audience sharing every event of the story with the actors.

HISTORY AND SIGNIFICANCE

Struggle between the forces of good and evil, and the eventual victory of the former over the latter, is the basic theme of *Ramayana*. Rama symbolizes the best in humanity and Ravana the evil forces.

Dussehra in Sanskrit means ten sins which are respresented in Ravana's ten heads and Rama destroys them. Ravana abducted Sita with the help of another demon named Maareecha. He kept Sita in the Ashoka Grove and persisted in making her his wife, but Sita always thought of her husband Rama. Rama sent his messengers to Ravana and urged him to return Sita. But the evil-minded Ravana refused to do so. Rama set off for Lanka with Sugriva, Hanuman, Angada, Jambvan and hundreds of other mighty monkeys. Ravana's younger brother Vibhishana, a noble soul and devotee of Lord Rama, however, took refuge under Rama. Rama built a causeway across the sea to carry him and his forces across the sea. Rama, along with his young brother Lakshmana, killed all the demons and their King Ravana and regained Sita. Finally they returned to Ayodhya in the 'Pushpak' viman.

PROCESSION

On this occasion huge effigies stuffed with brilliant fireworks are raised at various open grounds and set to fire by the one performing the role of Rama. The effigies are of Ravana, his brother Kumbhakarna and son Meghnada. This marks the culmination and termination of the celebrations. Elaborate and gorgeous processions depicting various scenes of the *Ramayana* in the form of tableau are taken out through *bazaars* and main streets. Apart from all this, *Ramlila* is also performed as a dance-drama by professional troupes.

Dussehra festival held at Mysore is one of India's most colourful phenomena. The spectacular procession taken out on this day is a veritable extravaganza. The colourful Dussehra fair and festival of Kullu is also very famous. Among the *Ramalilas*, the one staged at Varanasi is worth seeing.

CELEBRATIONS

On this auspicious day Lord Rama is worshipped, prayed and meditated upon to obtain his blessings and favour. In olden days, the kings used to march their forces against their enemies every year on this day, the day Rama routed Ravana. *Mithai*, fruits, *batashas*, etc., are served as *Prasad*.

KULLU DESSEHRA

While Dussehra is celebrated with great enthusiasm and fervour by burning effigies of Ravana, Kumbhkarna and Meghnada in various parts of the country, the unique Dussehra in the Kullu town of H.P. is a festival with a difference, devoid of such features.

conclude in other parts of the country and all activities revolve around the presiding deity "Lord Raghunathji".

The entire Kullu town, especially the sprawling Dhalpur Maidan which is converted into a temporary abode of Lord Raghunathji, vibrates with colourful celebrations with a strong blend of religious faith.

The festival begins with the arrival of the image of Goddess Hadimba from Manali and about 200 local "*Devtas*", accompanied by a host of attendants, who reach the venue in colourfully decorated palanquins to pay homage to Lord Raghunathji.

The image of Lord Raghunathji is brought from Sultanpur temple located in the palace of erstwhile Raja of Kullu and taken in a procession. All the local *'Devtas'* join the procession and devotees pull the ropes of flower-bedecked chariot of Lord Raghunathji as it is considered auspicious and brings fortune and prosperity.

There is no *Ram Lila* or burning of effigies of Ravana, his brother and son, but five animals are sacrificed on the last day at the banks of Beas river as "Lanka Dahan" (burning of Lanka) was performed on the same day.

The Goddess Hadimba returns to her abode Manali after *'Lanka Dahan'* and Lord Raghunathji also returns to the temple. The local *'Devtas'* also leave Dhalpur for their respective villages as the curtain falls on the festival.

The festival has been declared an international event by the state government and colourful cultural programmes by local, state, national and international troupes mark the evenings.

While the religious faith and devotion of people add serenity to the festival during morning hours, mirth and excitement mark the evenings.

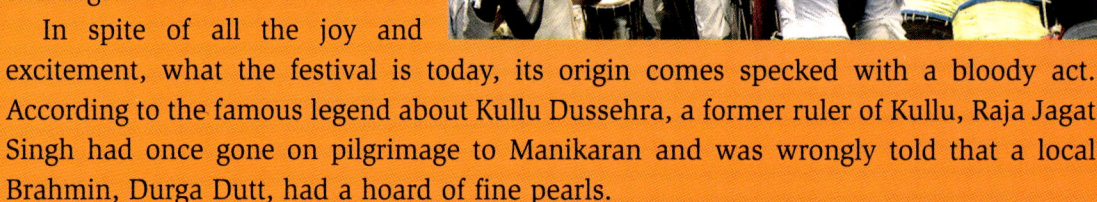

In spite of all the joy and excitement, what the festival is today, its origin comes specked with a bloody act. According to the famous legend about Kullu Dussehra, a former ruler of Kullu, Raja Jagat Singh had once gone on pilgrimage to Manikaran and was wrongly told that a local Brahmin, Durga Dutt, had a hoard of fine pearls.

He sent his men to ask Dutt if he would sell some of the pearls. When the Brahmin said he had no such pearls, the king's men started beating him and to escape the rain of blows, the Brahmin said he would give the pearls when the Raja returned from Manikaran.

When the king returned, his men again went to the Brahmin who locked himself and his family in the house and set it ablaze. When the house was engulfed by flames, Dutt climbed to the roof and started inflicting wounds on his body with a sharp-edged knife.

"You want pearls, here are the pearls", he cried and threw pieces of flesh from his body. Raja Jagat Singh, who watched the horrible scene, lost his peace of mind after some time and was not able to perform his duties.

Later, a holy man met him and advised him that the only way to get relief was to get the image of "Lord Raghunathji" from Ayodhya and worship it. Satisfied with Raja Jagat Singh's remorse, the holy man sent one of his disciples to Ayodhya to bring the image of Lord Raghunathji.

On arrival of the image, the Raja and his family paid homage to the deity and he declared that, henceforth, it will be the righteous rule of Raghunathji in the kingdom while he and his descendants would only act as regents.

Govardhan Puja

Goverdhan Puja is celebrated on Pratipada, i.e. the first day of the bright fortnight of Kartik (October-November), the day following Deepawali. Annakut is also observed on the same day. This day is associated with an interesting event in the life of Lord Krishna. On this day Krishna lifted the Govardhan mountain (in Vrindavan) on his little finger for seven days and protected the cows, and the people of Vrindavan against the deluge of rain sent by the enraged Indra, the god of heaven and rain.

It so happened that one day Krishna saw the people of Vrindavan making great preparations for the worship of Indra. Krishna convinced them of its futility and induced them to worship mount Govardhan, which provided shelter to them and nourishment to their cows. Accordingly they performed a great ceremony to honour the mountain and were amply rewarded by the manifestation of Krishna as the spirit of Govardhan. It enraged Indra, and he sent a terrible deluge to teach a lesson to the cowherds of Nandgaon and Vrindavan. It was then that Krishna raised the mountain and protected them under it for seven days and nights. Ultimately, Indra realized who Krishna really was. His pride was humbled and he came to Krishna in real humility and paid him homage.

Even today, people in thousands visit, worship and circumambulate Mount Govardhan on this day. Those who cannot come to Vrindavan worship it at their respective homes with great devotion and give gifts to Brahmins. Cows and bulls are also decorated and worshipped on this day.

Guru Parab

The Guru Parab falls on the full moon day of Kartik (October-November) and is celebrated to commemorate the birth of Guru Nanak, the founder Guru of Sikhism.

HISTORY AND SIGNIFICANCE

The birth anniversary of Guru Nanak Dev – the first Guru of the Sikhs, is celebrated with great fervour on the full moon day of Kartika. Guru Parab, also known as Jyototsava, is one of the most sacred festivals of the Sikhs.

Guru Nanak was born in 1469 at Talwandi, about 45 kms away from Lahore, now known as Nankana Sahib. At Nankana Sahib there is a beautiful Gurudwara, and a holy tank or *sarovar*. On Guru Parab, a grand fair and festival is held here, and Sikhs in thousands congregate here from India and abroad.

Guru Granth Sahib, the holy scripture, is continuously read and recited in the Gurudwaras *('Akhand path')* all over the country, lamps are lighted, processions are taken out, free *langars* (community meals) are arranged and *prasad* (holy food) is distributed. *Pandals* are set up in various places and *'prasad'* is distributed. Guru Parab celebrations at the Golden Temple in Amritsar, Punjab, are impressive.

Nanak was a great reformer, preacher and a saint. In Sikhism he tried to harmonize both Hinduism and Islam. He never believed in caste-distinctions and liberalized social practices. He preached the significance of God, for him faith in God was a potent means of spiritual realization. He believed that a persistent remembrance of God will help us to develop the best in us. A true Sikh strives not for salvation or paradise but always loves to see God. Many of Nanak's hymns, which form part of the *Guru Granth Sahib*, reflect clearly how the sight of God and his love itself is supreme.

Sikhs were to be distinguished by their name, always with the suffix Singh (lion), and by the five K's : uncut hair *(Kesh)*, comb *(Kangha)*, steel bangle on the right wrist *(Kada)*, short drawers *(Kachha)* and dagger *(Kirpan).*

God is both *nirgun* and *sagun.* Before creation, God lived absolutely nirgun but then he became *sagun* and manifested himself and became God or the Almighty; and in order to realize Himself, He made nature, which is his main abode and is diffused everywhere and in all directions in the form of love.

Nanak travelled widely in India and abroad and his life and teachings have been a great source of inspiration. Nine other human Gurus followed him in succession, under whom Sikhism gradually developed. Finally, the *Guru Granth Sahib* was declared as the eternal *Guru.*

TEACHINGS OF GURU NANAK

He was not only the founder of the Sikh religion, he was also a great poet, philosopher, humanist and a powerful social reformer, a teacher of mankind. Nanak said that one need not become a *sanyasi,* sacrificing one's family life, to please God. Those who practise devotion, whose minds are pure and who have sympathy, patience and honesty, are in no way inferior to a *sanyasi.* He considered that all human beings were highborn; no one was low.

CELEBRATIONS

On the day of Guru Parab, the holy scripture, *Guru Granth Sahib,* is continuously read and recited in the Gurudwaras. True worship consists in singing God's praises, in meditating on His name and so also are all pilgrimages and ascetical practices like fasting and celibacy. God is the Supreme Guru, 'Satnam, Wahe Guru'. The ten Gurus are revered because God spoke through them. The festival is observed with great enthusiasm all over India.

Similarly other Gurus are also commemorated on other Guru Parab days. For example, the other Guru Parab commemorating Guru Govind Singh is celebrated in the month of Paush (December-January).

Free sweets and *langars* or community lunches are also offered to everyone irrespective of one's religious faith. Men, women and children participate in *Kar Sewa* as service to the communtiy by participating in activities to cook food and distribute it in the *Guru Ka langar* with the traditional *Karah Prasad.*

PROCESSION

The day marks the culmination of *Prabhat Pheris*, the early morning processions, that start from the Gurudwaras and then go around localities singing *shabads* (hymns). On the day of the festival the *Granth Sahib* is also carried in a procession on a float, decorated with flowers, throughout the village or city. Five armed guards, who represent the Panj Piaras, lead the procession carrying *Nishan Sahib* (the Sikh flag). Local bands playing religious music form a special part of the procession.

PRABHAT PHERI

A few days before Guru Parab, people take out *Prabhat Pheris* or the early morning processions from the Gurudwaras. They go around their locality singing *shabad* or the religious hymns.

LANGAR

Later in the day, special *kirtans* are arranged in the Gurudwaras. The devotees attend *langar* or the community meals where everyone eats the same food irrespective of caste, or creed. Devotees offer their services for cooking food, cleaning the Gurudwara or carrying out other chores. This is called the *Kar Seva*.

ILLUMINATION

In the evening, the Gurdwaras are illuminated and people visit them in large numbers. People also illuminate their homes with candles and earthen lamps.

Kartik Purnima

Sikhs celebrate Kartik Purnima as Guru Parab and Nanak's birthday, but the Hindus celebrate it as a day when God incarnated himself as '*Matsya*' or Fish. Vishnu took the Fish incarnation to save Vaivasvata, the seventh Manu and the progenitor of the human race from the deluge.

It is also believed that Shankar killed demon Tripurasura on this day and so he is also called Tripurari.

CELEBRATIONS

Charities done and piety observed on this day are believed to earn high religious merit. Bathing in the Ganges, or in other holy waters is considered to be of special religious significance. People keep fast, practise charities and meditate on God.

Shiva is worshipped on this occasion and giving away of a bull (bull is the mount of Shiva) as a gift to a Brahmin, is thought to be of great religious significance. Big cattle fairs are also held on this day at various places. For example, the cattle fair held at the sacred Pushkar Lake, near Ajmer, is a great draw, which transforms the scene into a raving sea of colour and gaiety, tempered by the presence of a huge number of devotees. Thousands of camels, cows, bulls, buffaloes, sheep, goats etc., are brought there for sale. Camel race is held and gaeity, fun and merry-making mark the occasion. Over a hundred thousand pilgrims take bath there on this day in the sacred lake.

Kartik Snan

Among the twelve months of the year, some are regarded specially holy and sacred, and as such, most suitable for the acts of piety. These are Vaisakh, Kartik and Magha.

SIGNIFICANCE

Throughout the month of Kartik, the early morning bath in some river, stream, pond or at a well is considered highly meritorious. On the sacred rivers like Ganga, Yamuna etc., a month long bathing festival is held. Some people camp near the banks of rivers for this purpose, and at the termination of the month-long bathing festival they return to their distant homes. During the month the aspirants observe strict continence, have regular morning bath in the sacred streams, take a single simple meal every day and spend their time in prayer, meditation and acts of piety and devotion.

RITUAL

Womenfolk in villages and towns get up quite early in the morning, and go to the sacred streams in groups, singing hymns and, after ablutions, visit the nearby temples. They observe fast and hang lamps in small baskets, from the bamboo tops at their houses or on the riverbanks. These lamps are kept burning all through the month of Kartik to light the path of departed souls across the sky. *Tulsi* is also worshipped in the evening, and an earthen lamp is placed near it.

Tulsi plant is sacred to all Hindus and is kept planted in a pot in homes and temples. It is considered to be the wife of Vishnu and shown respect accordingly. The women worship it by lighting a lamp near it. Watering, cultivating and worshipping of *Tulsi* plant ensure happiness. When its leaves are put into any water it becomes as pure as *Gangaajal*. *Tulsi* leaves offered to Vishnu in the month of Kartik (November) pleases him more than the gift of a thousand cows.

Tulsi is generally grown on a small square pillar, hollow at the top, with its four sides facing the four cardinal directions. Since *Tulsi* is *Vishnupriya* (beloved of Vishnu), their marriage is celebrated during Kartik Shukla Ekadashi, i.e., the eleventh day of the bright half of Kartik (October-November). In *Padma Puran* we find the details of the ceremony. On this day *Tulsi* was married to Vishnu. The image of Vishnu is richly decorated and then carried to the place where *Tulsi* plant is grown, and there the marriage is ritually solemnized. Fast is observed on this day.

Karwa Chauth

The fast of Karwa Chauth is observed 9 days before Diwali. It falls on the fourth day of the Kartik month by the Hindu calendar (fourth day of the waning moon or the dark fortnight).

Karva Chauth is observed by married women (suhagin) for ensuring wedded bliss and wishing long life for their husbands and children.

THE RITUAL

Karwa Chauth is considered one of the most important fasts observed by the married Hindu women. On this day the women pray for the welfare and long life of their husbands. The festival is followed mainly in the northern parts of the country.

Married women eat some fruits and sweets early in the morning, well before sunrise. They are not supposed to eat or even drink a drop of water during the day. In the evening the ladies listen to the *Karwa Chauth Katha* (the legend). The fast is over after the moonrise.

THE PUJA PROCESS

The *pooja* preparations start a day in advance. Married women buy the *shringar* or the traditional adornments and the other *pooja* items like the *karwa*, *matthi*, *henna* etc.

Early in the morning they have some fruits and sweets before sunrise. The morning passes by in other festive activities like decorating hand and feet with *henna*, decorating the *pooja thali* and meeting friends and relatives.

In the late afternoon women gather at a common place like temple or a garden or someone's place who has arranged the *pooja*. An elderly lady or the *pujarin* narrates the legend of Karwa Chouth.

The essentials of this gathering and listening of the Karwa Chauth story are: a special clay pot that is considered a symbol of lord Ganesha, a metal urn filled with water, flowers, idols of Ambika Gaur Mata, Goddess Parvati and some fruits, *mathi* and foodgrains. A part of this is offered to the deities and the storyteller.

On the occasion of this *vrat* (fast) a *kalash* (small container) is filled with either milk or water. In that *kalash* is placed *Pancha Ratna* (five pieces of different metals–gold, silver, copper, brass and iron). The *kalash* is then presented to a Brahmin and also exchanged with other married women. While thus presenting the *kalash*, a wishful prayer is offered to Lord Ganesh: "Let the offerings of this *Karwa* bring long life to my husband and may my *suhag* be everlasting". And they also express such desire as: 'May my death precede that of my husband so that I can enter the *chitaa* (funeral pyre) as a *Suhagin*, not as a widow.'

Earlier an idol of Gaur Mata was made using earth and cow dung. Now just an idol of Goddess Parvati is kept. Everyone lights an earthen lamp in the *thalis* while listening to the Karwa Choth story. *Sindoor*, incense sticks and rice are also kept in the *thali*.

At this time the women wear heavy *saris* or *chunries* in red, pink or other bridal colours, and adorn themselves with all other symbols of a married woman like nose pin, *tika*, *bindi*, *chonp*, bangles, earrings etc.

Once the moon rises, the women see its reflection in a *thali* of water, or through a *dupatta* or a sieve. They offer water to the moon and seek blessings. They pray for the safety, prosperity and long life of their husbands. This marks the end of the day long fast.

LEGENDS

This *katha* (narrative) first took place between Siva and Parvati. Siva told Parvati about the significance of *Karwa Vrat*. In *Dwapar Yuga*, Draupadi asked Lord Krishna about the *vrat* of *Karwa Chauth*. Thereafter, the very first time Veeravati, the daughter of Vedsharma and Leelavati observed this *vrat* in the town of Shukraprastha. Ever since this *vrat* has been observed by married women till the present day.

On the occasion of Karwa Chauth which is on the day of Kartik Krishna Chaturthi, fasting *(vrat)* is observed. In the evening, after taking a bath, place under a banyan tree (or in the absence of such tree, a picture of such a tree can be drawn) *murtis* or pictures of Siva, Parvati, Ganesh and Kartikeya and do *puja* ceremony. Then for the offerings of *arghya* (rice, flower etc.), while waiting for the moon to rise, *japa* is done with the *mantra* "Om namah Shivaya". *Havan* (sacred fire ceremony) is also done. Thereafter, having sighted the moon, *arghya* is offered.

Husband is worshipped with *gandh*, *pushpa*, *dhoop*, *deep* and *naivedya* (perfume, flower, incense, lamp and food).

Lord Krishna urged Draupadi to observe the *vrat* of *Karwa Chauth* so that through its influence, Arjuna can defeat the Kauravas on the battlefield and acquire back the kingdom.

Married women who thus offer wishful prayer for *suhag* by observing the *Karwa Chauth Vrat*, acquire *suhag*, progeny and lasting prosperity.

Narak Chaturdashi

The next day to Dhan Teras is celebrated as Narak Chaturdashi. This day is dedicated to Yama, the god of Naraka or Hell. The early morning bath on this day is considered to be of great religious merit. It is believed that those who bathe on this *Tithi* after the sunrise get their religious merit destroyed. Therefore, people get up early in the morning and first of all have their ablutions, etc. Before bathing, oil is rubbed on the body, which is greatly invigorating and purifying.

After the bath, Yamraj is offered libations thrice to please and appease him, so that he may spare the person from the tortures of hell. Fast is observed and in the evening lamps are lit in honour of Yama. It is believed that piety observed on this day in honour of Lord Yama liberates a man from possible future tortures in hell.

Pitra Paksha

The dark half of the Ashvin (September-October) is observed as Pitra Paksha throughout the Hindu world, and sacrifices called 'Shraddh' are offered to the dead and departed ancestors of the family. On each day of the fortnight, oblations of water and *Pindas* or balls of rice and meal are offered to the dead relatives by the surviving relatives. A *Shraddh* is not a funeral ceremony but a supplement to such a ceremony. It is an act of reverential homage to a dead person, performed by relatives. It is believed that the performance of *Shraddh* after the funeral rites will supply the dead with strengthening nutriment. It is believed that until *Shraddh* has been performed the deceased is a restless soul. Only after the *Shraddh*, he attains a position among the *Pitras* or ancestors in their blissful abode called *Pitra-lok*. A *Shraddh* is most desirable and efficacious when done by a son.

The eldest son or some other elder male member of the family performs *Shraddh* in honour of the dead and offers oblation. Part of the food-offering is also given to the cows, dogs and crows. Brahmins are fed and given *daan-dakshina*, for it is believed that whatever is given to the Brahmins also reaches the departed souls. *Kheer*, a sweet dish made of milk and rice, is specially prepared and offered for the *Pitras* on this occasion. On the last day of the fortnight, i.e. *Amavasya* oblations are offered to all those dead ancestors whose date of death is not known. In *Brahma Puran* the significance of this ceremony is described. During Pitra Paksha shaving of the beard, cutting of the hair, wearing of new clothes, cutting of the nails etc, are not allowed.

Sharad Purnima

Sharad Purnima is observed on the night of full moon of *Ashvin*. *Ashvin* is also known as Moon-god and the lord of herbs, seeds, the Brahmins, water and *Nakshatras* or constellations. It is believed that on the Sharad Purnima, Moon throws its beams showering *Amrit* or elixir on the earth.

CELEBRATIONS

On this auspicious day *Ksheer* or *Kheer* (milk thickened with rice and mixed with sugar) is specially prepared in the temple and homes, and offered to Hari amidst ringing of bells and chanting of hymns, then it is given in the morning as *Prasad* to the devotees. The *kheer* is kept in moonshine the whole night so that it may absorb the *Amrit* falling from the moon. Such *Kheer* is considered to possess many qualities. At night Moon-god is also worshipped and offered *naivedya*.

Skanda Shashthi

Skanda Shasthi is celebrated in South India with great religious fervour and devotion in the Tamil month of Tulam (October-November).

HISTORY AND SIGNIFICANCE

Skanda is the second son of Shiva, and is also known as Karttikeya or Subramanya. He was born without the intervention of a female. Shiva cast his seed into the fire, and Goddess Ganga received it afterwards. Krithikas, wives of six sages, fostered him and hence he got six heads and the name Karttikeya. He was born for the purpose of destroying Taraka, a demon whose austerities had made him formidable to gods.

Karttikeya is represented riding a peacock, holding a bow in one hand and an arrow in the other. His wife is Devasena or Kumari. He is known by many titles – as a warrior he is known as Mahasena or Senapati; Siddha-sena, 'leader of the Siddhas'; Yuddha-rang; Kumar, 'the boy'; Guha, 'the mysterious one'; Shakti-dhara, 'the spear holder' and in the south he is called Subramanya. He is also called, Dwadashahara (twelve-handed) Dwadasksha (twelve-eyed).

CELEBRATIONS

In south India there are six places, which are associated with his life and hence regarded most holy. At all these places Skanda Shashthi is celebrated with great fervour and thousands of devotees congregate at each temple to seek the Lord's blessings.

RITUAL

Skanda Shashthi is the commemoration of the day on which Taraka was defeated. *Bhajans* are sung, *Kirtans* chanted, and scenes from his life are dramatized on the occasion. The festivity begins six days preceding the Shashthi. Lord Subramanya is worshipped during these days and devotees set on pilgrimage to various shrines of Subramanya.

SIGNIFICANCE

The piety and devotion observed on this day ensures success, prosperity, peace and happiness. In the *Gita*, Sri Krishna has said: "Among the generals of armies, I am Karttikeya".

Surya Shashti

The fast of Surya Shashti is observed on the sixth day of the bright fortnight of Kartik (October-November).

CELEBRATIONS

Married women having children observe this fast which lasts for three days. A day earlier i.e. on the day of Panchami, meal is taken only once and that too without salt. On the next day, i.e. on Shashti, women on fast do not take even water and worship the sun with *naivedya* and water and keeps a night vigil.

The next day, that is on the *Saptami* day, the aspirant women bathe early at the bathing *ghats*, before sunrise and then break their fast. Brahmins are given food and gifts on this day. It is believed that the fast and piety observed on this day ensure good health, longevity and happiness of their husband and children.

Valmiki Jayanti

The birthday of the Adi Kavi (the First Poet) Valmiki is celebrated on the full moon day of Ashvin (September-October).

SIGNIFICANCE

Valmiki is the author of the great epic *Ramayana* in Sanskrit. He was a contemporary of Rama, the hero of *Ramayana*. Valmiki himself is represented as taking part in some of the scenes he relates. He received the banished Sita into his hermitage and educated her twin sons Luv and Kush.

HISTORY

Originally, Valmiki belonged to a depressed class and led the life of a brigand. He killed the people passing through the forest, but because of the influence of some sages, he repented and betook himself to a hermitage on a hill in the district of Banda in Bundelkhand. It is there that he eventually sheltered Sita, when banished by Rama.

He got his name '*Valmiki*' because once he was so immersed in meditation, that he allowed himself to be covered by ants which almost formed an anthill. His original name was Ratnakar. Many depressed classes in the country trace their lineage to Valmiki.

CELEBRATIONS

On his birthday he is worshipped and prayed and his portraits are taken out in processions through the main *bazaars* and streets. *Kirtans* are also held in Valmiki temples.

Guru Gobind Singh Jayanti

Celebrated by the Sikhs, the birthday of their tenth and last human Guru, this day witnesses large processions and special prayer gatherings at all Gurudwaras.

BACKGROUND

Guru Gobind Singh, the tenth Sikh Guru, was born at Patna Sahib on December 22, 1666 (*Poh Sudi Saptmi*). His birthday generally falls in December or January or sometimes twice within a year as it is calculated according to Hindu Bikrami Calendar, which is based on the lunar calendar. According to the Nanakshahi Calendar, the birthday of Guru Gobind Singh falls on January 5.

AN OVERVIEW OF GURU GOBIND SINGH'S LIFE

Guru Gobind Singh (1666-1708 C.E.) lived during an extremely dangerous time. His father, Guru Teg Bahadur, sacrificed his life to protect the freedom of worship by Hindus, who were being threatened with conversion by Muslim rulers. Abduction of women and pillage of goods were rampant, but the people were too timid to resist. In the midst of this political situation, Guru Gobind Singh gained great stature as both, a saint and a leader with spiritual principles and intense devotion to God, and at the same time, fearless dedication to protection of people from oppression and injustice through the practice of *Kshetradharma*.

In 1699, he dramatically initiated five men as His five Beloved with great courage as well as nearness to God. They became models for the Sikh fraternity naming it *Khalsa* meaning *Pure*, which Guru Gobind Singh created to stand on the front line against injustice, held to a very strict moral and spiritual discipline and under Guru Gobind Singh's inspiration, helped to turn the tide against Mughal oppression in India.

In addition to his spiritual and military leadership, Guru Gobind Singh wrote on spiritual issues which infused a martial spirit in the people.

This included the *Jap Sahib*, but he did not include them in the Sikh scripture, the *Guru Granth Sahib* but made a separate volume, called the *Dasam Granth*. Before his passing away, he instructed that the *Guru Granth Sahib* be regarded their teacher. '*Granth*' literally means 'volume' (especially, a holy volume) of reverence used for anything sacred. The *Guru Granth Sahib* is the perpetual Guru of the Sikhs today.

Vaitarani Vrata

It is observed on the eleventh day of the dark half of Margashirsha (November-December). The faithful observe fast and other rituals, as prescribed, on this day. In the evening a black cow is worshipped. It is bathed in fragrant water, and sandalwood paste is applied on its horns and then *naivedya* is offered. Brahmins are also given gifts of food, raiment and a cow made of either gold or silver.

The river *Vaitarani*, the Hindu Styx, is to be crossed by the departed souls before entering the infernal region. The river is said to be filled with all kinds of filth, blood, odour, etc. It flows with great impetuosity and can be crossed only with the help of a cow. That is why a cow is worshipped and offered *naivedya* on this day. A cow given to a Brahmin is considered an act that will help one cross the river easily after death. Therefore, cows are given in charity to Brahmins at the time of one's death.

Kumbha Parva

Kumbha means a pitcher or a water pot. In the beginning of the creation, the gods, under the curse of Rishi Durvasa, were defeated by the demons and turned out of their abode (heaven). They went to Vishnu and sought his help. He advised them to churn the ocean for *Amrit* or elixir. When the *Amrit Kumbha* (pitcher of nectar) appeared in the process of churning, there ensued a scramble between the gods and the demons, and some of its contents splashed out and fell at four places.

These four places are Hardwar or Haridwar, Prayag (Allahabad), Ujjain and Nasik. Now, Kumbha Parva or Mela is held once in every 12 years by rotation, at these places. It is called *Purn Kumbha*, and the one held once in every six years, after the full ones, is called the *Ardh Kumbha* (half *Kumbha*). At Haridwar it lasts for about a month and a half of Phalguna-Chaitra, when the sun passes to Aries, and Jupiter is in Aquarius. At Prayag, it is held in the month of Magh (January-February), when Jupiter is in Aries, and the sun and the moon in Capricorn. The Ujjain Kumbha is held in the month of Kartik (October-November), when these planets are in Libra. It is held at Nasik on the banks of Godavari, in the month of Shravan (July-August), when these planets are in Cancer. These Kumbha melas terminate with the final bath on the new moon day.

Kumbha Mela is the most magnificent bathing festival ever held in the world. Millions of people, which include saints, *sanyasis, rishi-munis*, priests, *naga sadhus, mahants* and laymen from all parts of the country, participate in it. Sometimes, the rush of devotees is so unmanageable that in spite of great preparations for several months ahead, there is a stampede, and the result is a mass tragedy. In the *Kumbha Mela*, held at Haridwar in March-April 1986, at least 100 pilgrims died and scores were injured. And it was not for the first time. The toll was much larger on earlier occasions. There were two mishaps when more than 500 and more than 18000 pilgrims are said to have perished.

It is believed that the Jupiter, the Sun and the Moon helped in protecting the *Amrit Kumbha* from being snatched by the demons; hence, the position of these three planets determine the principal bathing dates. During *Kumbha Mela*, there are continuous recitation and reading of scriptures, epics and *Purans*. Religious discourses are held; food, clothing, money and other gifts are given liberally to the needy and to saints and *sadhus*. The day is marked by endless processions of *mahants* in richly decorated swinging palanquins; of ash-smeared *naga* (naked) sadhus and of sages with their matted locks, either dangling loose around their heads or tied into a knot above the head. A holy dip during Kumbha Parva is highly meritorious, as it destroys all sins. The ancient Hindu scriptures wax eloquently in praise of these fairs. These reflect the true soul of India, the glory and greatness that India possessed/possesses and the living faith enshrined in the hearts of millions and millions of Hindus.

Mal-Mas

Mal-mas is also called *Adhikmas* or *Purushottam-mas*. It is an intercalated 13th month. The month in which the sun does not move from one position or sign into the other is called *Mal-mas*. It occurs after every 32 months, 13 days and 4 *ghatis*. And the month in which the sun passes into another sign or position twice is known as *Kshaya-mas*. First it occurs after 141 years and then after 19 years.

SIGNIFICANCE AND CELEBRATIONS

During *Mal-mas* religious ceremonies are prohibited. Fasts observed and charities practised during *Mal-mas* are said to be highly meritorious and these destroy sins. During *Mal-mas ghee*, grains and jaggery should be given to the Brahmins daily, in charity. Anspicious ceremonies like marriages are not performed during the *Mal-mas*, but libations and oblations are specially offered to the dead ancestors and *Pretas* (ghosts).

When *Mal-mas* occurs either in the month of Vaishakha, or Jyaishtha or Ashad, it is considered to be inauspicious. In the rest of the months it is always good. During *Mal-mas* a grand fair is held at Rajgriha (once the capital of Magadha), in Bihar. According to *Purans* at that time, 33 crore gods and goddesses descend there, and it turns the place into the most sacred place and centre of pilgrimage on the earth.

Mangalvar Vrata

It is a popular fast, and is observed to propitiate Mahavir Hanuman, who rendered great service to Lord Rama. He acted as his spy and fought most valiantly. He helped in restoring Lakshmana back to life by bringing medicinal herbs from the Himalayas. He accompanied Rama to Ayodhya and there he received from him the boon of perpetual life and youth. There is no other deity so helpful in the times of difficulty.

CELEBRATIONS

On Tuesdays strict fast is kept, and Hanuman is worshipped with sweets and fruits and *Hanuman Chalisa* is read and recited. The idols of Hanuman are coated with vermilion colour mixed in *Ghee* on this day. After *puja*, *prasad* (sweet) is distributed and only then the fast is broken. Only one meal is taken on this day and that too without salt. On Tuesdays, fairs are held at many places near the Hanuman temples. Observing of *Mangalvar Vrata* ensures success, happiness, strength–both physical and moral, and quick recovery from illness. It also helps in overcoming the enemies.

Pradosha Vrata

*P*radosha means the dusk or the early night or evening tide. This vow is observed in the evening twilight, and so it is called *Pradosha Vrata*. It is observed on the 13th day of each lunar fortnight. It is practised to propitiate Lord Shiva, in order to obtain his blessings and boons leading to fulfilment of one's cherished desires and spiritual upliftment. The evening tide, when the sun sets and the night approaches, is the best time to worship Shiva.

A thing practised at an opportune moment is likely to bear the best possible results. That is why there is so much emphasis on observing rituals, ceremonies, vows etc. on a given day at a given hour. Our seers have ordained *Pradosha* vow to be practised in the evening, because then it is most efficacious. The gods themselves approached Lord Shiva once at the most auspicous moment of *Pradosha* to seek succour in the hour of distress, when they were being harassed and tormented by the *Danavas* and *Daityas*. And they were quite successful in achieving Mahadeva's favours and blessings.

This fast is highly praised in the *Purans*, and is of great religious merit. Those who practise it with unflinching faith and devotion are bound to possess wealth, health, happiness and peace of mind. When *Pradosha* falls on either Monday, Saturday or Sunday, it is considered all the more auspicious.

CELEBRATIONS

An aspirant should get up early at dawn on *Pradosha* day and, having finished his daily and regular ablution, should invoke Shiva and meditate on him. On that day he should not eat anything, Then, again at the time of *Pradosha*, he should bathe and purify himself, and put on clean clothes and sit for ritual worship in a sanctified place. He should, preferably, sit on a seat of *kusha* grass, facing east, but never facing west or south. Then he should offer *Shodashopachar Puja* (16 acts of homage) to Shiva with seasonal flowers, *bael* leaves, fruit, lamps, incense, etc.

To offer even one such *Pradosha puja* equals in merit to scores of other *pujas*. To light even a single Ghee lamp at such auspicious moments is highly rewarding. Along with Shiva, Parvati, Ganesh, Karttikeya and the Nandi Bull are also worshipped and *Maha Mrityunjaya Mantra* is repeated 108 times. The priest and Brahmin should be given clothes, grains, a pitcher and money at the conclusion of the ceremony. While breaking the fast only light meal, consisting of fruits, curd, sweets, etc, should be taken. Night vigil should be kept and *Pradosha stotra* from the *Skanda Purana* should be read and recited.

Satyanarayana Vrata

This *Vrata* can be observed either on *Sankranti*, *Ekadashi* or *Amavasya* or *Puranmasi*. But in Northern India, it is generally observed on the full moon day (*Puranmasi*) of every month.

SIGNIFICANCE

Satyanarayana or *Satyadeva* means the Lord of Truth, and it is another name of Vishnu. The merits obtained by observing this *Vrata* are many. It destroys all sins and evils, and ensures peace of mind, bliss, prosperity, happy relations, health and truthfulness. In *Kaliyuga*, worship of Lord Satyanarayana with devotion is like the attainment of the veritable wishfulfilling cow.

HISTORY

There are many interesting legends in connection with the observance of this fast.

Once Devrishi Narada happened to visit the earth, also known as the *Mrityuloka*. He was very much distressed to find the misery, ill-health and poverty that haunted the inhabitants of earth. He wanted to relieve the sufferings of the mankind, but could not find out any way. He went to *Satyaloka* and told all about it to Bhagwan Satyanarayana. Lord Narayana advised Narada to inform the mankind to observe Satyanarayana fast on the day of *Purnima* or *Ekadashi*, *Amavasya* or *Sankranti* which would get rid of all evils, sins and sufferings and would ensure prosperity, happiness and bliss.

Narada returned to the earth and preached the importance of *Satyanarayana Vrata*. People did accordingly. They observed strict fast and meditated on him, and had all their desires fulfilled.

There is another story, which very beautifully underlines the spiritual significance of observing a vow on this day: There was a very poor Brahmin. He lived on alms and spent his days in misery. One day Lord Satyanarayana took pity, and appeared before him in the guise of a learned Brahmin (*Pandit*). The Load ordained him to observe the *Satyanarayana Vrata*. The next day was *Puranmasi*. He prepared a simple *bhog* of baked flour and sugar, and

SATYANARAYANA VRATA 173

after worhipping Narayana with full devotion and faith, distributed the *prasad*, and partook of it and prospered.

On the next *Puranmasi*, he celebrated the fast on a grand scale. A poor woodcutter chanced to pass by his house. The poor woodcutter heard the *Satyanarayana katha*, ate the *prasad*, and being inspired, observed the vow himself along with his wife and children, with complete devotion and piety, proper for the occasion. Consequently, he became very rich, enjoyed all the joys of life and after death attained the blissful abode of Lord Hari, the *Satyaloka*.

SIGNIFICANCE

Satyanarayana Vrata is the easiest and most inexpensive way of self-purification and self-surrender at the lotus feet of Hari. One who observes it with full devotion and faith is sure to attain wish fulfilment. Such a celebration creates healthy and pure vibrations and purges the heart of all dross and evil.

CELEBRATIONS

On this auspicious day, the aspirants should get up early in the morning and after taking bath they should pray and worship Suryanarayana first of all, and thereafter invoke him. They should make a small pavilion with plantain trunks, flowers, leaves, etc. and install therein picture of Satyanaryana. Then, the Lord should be ritually worshipped with camphor, fruits, lamps, incense, water, *naivedya*, betel leaf, etc., and the story of the *vrata* should be heard from a Brahmin. The Brahmin should be given gifts of grain, fruit, sweets, money, etc. and then *prasad* should be distributed. And finally in the afternoon the fast should be broken.

Shukravar Vrata

This vow is observed in several forms and is believed to be beneficial in many ways. It may be observed for the propitiation of the planet *Shukra*, and to ensure peace of mind and harmony in the family. It is also observed in honour of the goddess of wealth Lakshmi. Lakshmi is worshipped with white flowers, white raiments and *naivedya* prepared with *ghee* and sugar. In *Bhavishya Puran*, this vow is described in detail.

Nowadays, it is a very popular fast, and is observed by many women to please goddess Santoshi Mata. Santoshi Mata is another form of Parvati or Durga. Durga is known by thousands of names. She is *Dus Bhuja*, 'ten-armed'; *Singh-Vahini*– 'rides a lion'; *Mahisha-mardini*– 'destroyer of demon Mahisha'; *Kali*–'the black'; *Kanyakumari*– 'the youthful virgin'; *Ambika*– 'the mother'; *Sarvamangla*– 'always auspicious'; and so on.

As the *Shakti* or female energy of Shiva, she is both fierce and mild. As Santoshi Ma she is mild and gracious. On this day strict fast is observed and *jagaran* is done during night, and devotees sing her praises and glories in an assembly to the tune of music. In the morning *prasad* is distributed after final worship. Some devotees go to Vaishno Devi shrine in Jammu, after observing vow on Fridays. But it depends on one's inclination, means and capacity. *Santoshi Mata Vrata* can be observed individually without much pomp and show. A *vrata* is actually a matter of faith and devotion and hardly requires any exhibitionism.

Somvar Vrata

Somvar (Monday) fast is observed to propitiate Shiva and Parvati. The fast is terminated in the late afternoon and either fruits or light food is taken but only once. Some people observe it continuously for sixteen Mondays, and then terminate it with elaborate rituals and ceremony. The gift of a cow with its calf given to a Brahmin on this occasion is regarded to be highly meritorious.

During the month of Chaitra, Somvar vows are observed to please Jagannath, the Lord of Universe. Generally a person, who has been at least once to Jagannathpuri, is entitled to observe such a vow, but even if any one of the members of his family has been on a pilgrimage to Jagannath, he can undertake it. Lord Jagannath is ritually worshipped in the late afternoon and *naivedya* is offered. After the ritual, *prasad* is distributed and *dakshina* is given to the priest, and only then food is taken.

Vikram Samwat
(Months and Days)

Hindu fasts and festivals are generally based on Vikram Samwat. Named after King Vikramaditya, it came into being 57 years ahead of the Christian era. The Hindu year begins in *Chaitra* and counted from the *Samvatsara Parva*, the first day of the waxing moon in the month of *Chaitra*.

Seasons, months, fortnights and days under this system are as follows:

SEASONS	MONTHS
1. *Vasant* (Spring)	*Chaitra* (Mar- Apr), *Baisakh* (Apr-May)
2. *Greeshma* (Summer)	*Jyeshta* (May-June), *Ashadh* (June-July)
3. *Paavas* (Rainy Season)	*Shrawan/Savan* (Jul-Aug)
	Bhatrapad/Bhadon (Aug-Sep)
4. *Sharad* (Autumn)	*Ashwin* (Sep-Oct), *Kartik* (Oct-Nov)
5. *Hemant* (Mild Winter)	*Marg Shreersh* (Nov- Dec), *Paush* (Dec-Jan)
6. *Shishir* (Winters)	*Magh* (Jan-Feb), *Phalgun/ Phagun* (Feb-Mar)

FORTNIGHTS

Each fortnight is called *'Paksh'*. Bright fortnight, beginning with the new moon, is called *Shukla Paksh* and the dark fortnight is called *Krishna Paksh*.

DAYS (TITHI)

First day of the lunar fortnight *Pratipad*. Second day onwards are *Dwitiya, Tritiya, Chaturthi, Panchmi, Shashti, Saptmi, Ashtmi, Navmi, Dashmi, Ekadshi, Dwadashi, Triyodashi, Chaturdashi* and the fifteen day is *Purnima* in case of bright fortnight and *Amavasya* in case of dark fortnight. (Each day does not comprise of exactly 24 hrs and can vary and as such, a particular day of Hindu calendar can sometimes overlap 2 days or even miss a day of the Gregorian calendar.)

Fairs and Festivals of India
A Chronological List

The colourful mosaic of Indian festivals and fairs – as diverse as the land – is an expression of the spirit of celebration. Festivals are like gems, ornaments the crown of Indian culture. They are round-the-year vibrant interludes in the mundane routine of life. Every season brings along new festivals, each a true celebration, of the bounties of nature. And that's not all! The birthdays of gods and goddesses, saints and prophets, great historical happenings and the advent of the new year, all find expression in colourful festivities. The same festival, though celebrated differently in various parts of the country, exhibits an eternal harmony of spirit. Packed with fun and excitement, festivals are occasions to clean and decorate houses, to get together with friends and relatives and to exchange gifts. New attire, dance, music and rituals, all add to their joyful rhythm. It is a time for prayer, pageantry and processions, a time to rejoice.

Some of the major festivals, fairs and fasts have been listed here in chrological order for easy reference of readers:

MONTH	LOCATION	FESTIVALS
January	Gujarat	International Kite Festival
	Karnataka	Navarasapur- Pattadakkal
	Kerala	Great Elephant March
	Orissa	Beach Festival
	Pondicherry	Fete De Pondicherry/Yoga Festival
	Tamil Nadu	Tea and Tourism Festival, Coonoor
		Mahabalipuram Dance Festival, Pongal
	Rajasthan	Bikaner Camel Festival
	Punjab	Guru Gobind Singh Jayanti, Lohri
	All India	Makar Sankranti

Month	State	Festival
February	Goa	Goa Carnival
	Haryana	Surajkund Crafts Mela
	Karnataka	Coorg Festival
	Kerala	Nishagandhi Dance Festival
	Madhya Pradesh	Khajuraho Festival
	Maharashtra	Elephanta Festival
	Mizoram	Chapcharkut Festival
	Orissa	Konark Dance Festival
	Rajasthan	Desert Festival, Nagaur Festival
	Tamil Nadu	Natyanjali Festival, Chidambaram
	Uttar Pradesh	Taj Mahotsava, Agra
	Uttaranchal	Yoga Festival, Rishikesh
	All India	Mahashivratri
February/March	Andhra Pradesh	Deccan Festival
	Karnataka	Hoysala Mahotsav
	Bihar	Bihar Vaishali Mahotsava
	Gujarat	Somnath Festival
	Madhya Pradesh	Tansen Festival, Khajraho Dance Festival
	Kerala	Elephant Festival
	Punjab	Holla Mohalla
	All India	Holi
April/May	Rajasthan, Punjab, Haryana, Himachal Pradesh, Gujarat, Rajasthan	Gangaur, Mewar Festival, Baisakhi
		Mahavir Jayanti
	All India	Ram Naumi, International Flower Festival
June	Jammu & Kashmir	Ladakh Festival
	Orissa	Rath Yatra
July	All India	Naag Panchmi
	Jammu & Kashmir	Amarnath Yatra

HINDU FASTS & FESTIVALS

August	Bihar	Teej Festival
	Kerala	Boat Race
	All India	Janmashtami, Ganesh Chaturthi, Ganesh Festival
	Kerala	Onam
	All India	Durga Puja
October	Himachal Pradesh	Kullu-Dussehra Festival
	Madhya Pradesh	Pachmarhi Festival
	Nagaland	Autumn Festival
	Rajasthan	Cattle and Religious Fair
	Punjab, Haryana, Himachal Pradesh, Delhi	Karwa Chouth
	All India	Dussehra
November	Bihar	Sonpur Mela
	Chhotanagpur	Adivasi Mela
	Haryana	Kurukshetra Festival
	Rajasthan	Jhalawar Festival
	Uttar Pradesh	Avadh Festival (Lucknow)
Nov./Dec.	Goa	Goa Food and Cultural Festival
	Sikkim/W. Bengal	Teesta Tea and Tourism Festival
	Assam	Assam Tea Festival
	Chandigarh	Garden Festival
	Maharashtra	Ellora Festival
	Orissa	Konark Dance Festival
	Rajasthan	Shilpgram Crafts Mela
	West Bengal	Darjeeling Tea Festival, Vishnupur Festival

Glossary-Cum-Dictionary

Agni Deva – the Vedic god of Fire, instrumental in establishing contact between the worshipped and the worshipper

Annapurna – Goddess of Plenty (of grains), a benevolent form of goddess Parvati

Aryan – member of races speaking Indo-European or Indo-Germanic languages, who inhabited the Gangetic plains and built a great civilisation there

Atma – soul, the spiritual or immaterial part of living beings

Avtaar – Incarnation, an embodiment of eternal gods in mortal form, the most popular being the ten incarnations of Vishnu, of which nine have already appeared (including Rama, Krishna and Buddha) and the last one, Kalki, scheduled to appear sometime in near future (according to the popularly accepted ten-incarnations theory)

Ayurveda – originating in India during the Vedic times, it is a study of human body to remove imbalances between body's three basic forces knows as *Vat* (which controls body's physical and psychological rythms), *Pitt* (which controls heat and metabolism) and *Kaph* (which controls the overall structure and stability of the body)

Brahm Mahurt – a point in time, just before dawn, considered as the best time to wake up, an original day-light time saving concept later popularised by the West

Brahma – creator of the universe and one among the trinity of eternal Hindu gods, namely Brahma, Vishnu and Mahesh (Shiv)

Brahmand – cosmos, the whole and infinite creation, consisting of galaxies, living beings and all material things

Brahm – the supreme divinity, not to be confused with Brahma

Brahmin – or Brahman, the superior class in a caste classification among Hindus, who engage themselves in scholarly and religious activities

Brihaspati – counsellor of gods and their high priest

Buddha – the 9th incarnation of Vishnu and founder of Buddhism

Chitragupta – the record-keeper in heaven, for keeping record of good and bad deeds which facilitates decision making about sending people to heaven or hell, after death

Choti – tail of hair at the crown of the head, usually referring to the one kept by devout

Hindu males, particularly by the Brahmins

Cow – accorded a very high status by Hindus, its slaughter being banned (also read Kamdhenu)

Daan – alms, usually given to the poor

Dakshina – fees given to the priestly class, usually in kind, towards performance of religious rituals or to the teacher in lieu of the knowledge imparted

Dayanand Swami – the celebrated Hindu reformer who founded Arya Samaj in the late 19th century

Dhanvantri – the physician god who emerged during *Samudra Manthan*, holding a jar of medicines and *amrit* (read elixir)

Dharma – faith, belief in religious doctrines which provide a guide to character and conduct of humans

Duapar – 3rd of the four *yugas* during which Krishna appeared on earth as the 8th incarnation of Vishnu.

Durga – the fierce form or manifestation of goddess Parvati

Fasting – called *Vrat* or *Upvaas*, a scheme of imposing certain discipline on self, mainly on eating pattern, for a specified short time period

Ganesha – the elephant-headed god of auspicious beginnings and remover of obstacles

Ganga – the goddess represented by the holy river by the same name

Garuda – the vehicle of god Vishnu.

Gayatri Mantra – the sacred *Vedic* hymn in praise of the sun god *Surya*

Gita – better known as *Bhagwat Gita*, the most sacred Hindu scripture as the sermon given to Arjun by Krishna, during the *Mahabharata* war, about the importance of selfless performance of assigned duty

Gregorian Calendar – the prevalent English calendar first adopted in the UK in 1752, a modification of the earlier Julian calendar, to bring dates into closer conformity with astronomical data.

Guru – teacher, particularly a spiritual teacher

Hanuman – the monkey god, the god of power and strength, who helped Rama during his fight against Ravana

Havan – the ritual performed by offering some sacred items (like clarified butter, grains etc.) to fire in an effort to propitiate gods

Hindu – people living beyong (south and east of) river Sindhu (Indus) in the Indo-Gangetic plain, the word *Sindhu* distorted to *Hindu*, by Persians

Hindusim – the religion followed by Hindus as guided by religious scriptures like the *Vedas* (also see 'Sanatan Dharma')

Horoscope – a guiding document for individuals about the influence of planets and stars on a person's life and activities

Indra – the *Vedic* god, chief among smaller gods

Jagannath – a special form of Krishna, without hands and legs, installed in a temple in Puri in Orissa. Interestingly, the English word '*Juggernaut*' meaning notion or institution to which persons blindly sacrifice themselves or others, originates from *Jagannath*

Janeu – the sacred thread worn by Hindus on their body from the time they reach adolescence

Jhulelal – the 10th century popular saint of the Sindhi community, believed to be an incarnation of *vedic* god Varun

Kalki – the 10th incarnation of Vishnu, scheduled to appear in future, at the end of the present *Kalyug*, an era which began around the times of *Mahabharata* war

Kalyug – last of the four *yugas* and the currently on one, a time when righteousness in society is at the nadir

Kamdhenu – also called *Surabhi*, the celestial cow of plenty which emerged during *Samudra Manthan*

Kartikeya – the god of war and elder brother of Lord Ganesha

Krishna – the 8th incarnation of Lord Vishnu during *Duaparyuga* and the orator of *Gita* on the significance of *Karma* (duty)

Ksheer Sagar – ocean of milk where Lord Vishnu rests on the bed formed by coiling of Sheshnaag, with consort goddess Lakshmi

Kuber – the god of money and king of *Yakshas*, the spirits that reside in secluded forests, supposedly guarding hidden treasures

Kumbh Mela – large congregation of Hindu priests and other devotees taking ritual dip together in certain rivers at a pre-determined time of planetary alignments which happen four times every twelve years

Kurma – the divine tortoise as the 2nd incarnation of Lord Vishnu which appeared at the begininng of *Satyug*, to hold on its back the newly created globe (planet earth) and to help stabilize it

Lakshmi – the goddess of fortune and consort of Lord Vishnu

Legend – traditionally popular mythical stories

Lok – realm, like *Swarg Lok* (the realm of heaven)

Mahabharata – literally meaning *great India* but generallv referring to the war between Pandavas and Kauravas of the Kuru dynasty which occurred during *Duaparyuga*, with Krishna playing an important role in that war

Mahavira – the 24th *Teerthankar* (holy teacher/guide) of Jain community, who lived during 599-467 BC

Mala (or rosary) – a set of beads made of wood, cotton, pearl or *Rudraksh*, bound together with a thread to form a closed loop and used generally for facilitating concentration on god or to keep count of the *mantras*, number of beads being generally 108, a number considered auspicious as it relates to the 27 constellations in the entire zodiac, each constellation being made up of 4 phases, thus 27x 4 = 108 signifying coverage of the entire space, meaning greatness

Mantra – a collection of alphabets /words, usually pronounced musically, in praise of gods/goddesses or other divine beings

Matsya – the divine fish as the lst incarnation of Vishnu which appeared at the beginning of the current world, to take out the *Vedas* from the ocean to help Lord Brahma work on the cyclic process of creation of the universe

Mythology – collection of myths prevailing in a geographical area

Nakshatras – lunar mansions for charting heavens, a science which was known even in the *Vedic* times

Narak – hell where souls of the unrighteous are believed to be sent after death

Nandi – the sacred bull and vehicle of Lord Shiva

Narad – the celestial seer (*rishi*) as the messenger between gods

Narsimha – the 4th incarnation of Vishnu who appeared around the end of *Satyug*, to save his devotee Prahlad

Om – the mystic and holy hymn which sums up all the truth in the universe

Parashuram – the 6th incarnation of Vishnu who appeared at close of *Satyug*, to repress tyranny of powerful Kshatriyas of those times

Parvati – the goddess of fertility and consort of Lord Shiva

Pati Dev – a popularly accepted term used by Hindu women addressing husbands as *Pati Dev*, equating them with *Devas*, the gods

Plexus – network of nerve fibres in the body

Pralay – the great deluge and annihilation of the universe at the end of each cosmic cycle

Purans – religious literature giving tales pertaining to Hindu mythology

Rama – the 7th incarnation of Lord Vishnu, appeared during the *Tretayug* to give lessons in righteousness, to humanity

Ramayana – the epic describing the life and times of Lord Rama, scripted by Valmiki, sometime 500 BC

Ramcharit Manas – the Hindi version of Valmiki's *Ramayan* scripted by Tulsidas, a 16th century poet and saint

Rudraksh – a powerful and sacred seed, which is claimed to help one achieve physical, emotional and intellectual advantages as well as prosperity

Samudra Manthan – churning of the ocean jointly by gods and demons to extract nectar to achieve immortality. Fourteen entities are believed to have appeared during this churning process, including the divine cow *Surabhi*, the celestial tree *Parijat*, poison, goddess Lakshmi, the physician god Dhanvantri who carried with him a jar containing divine medicines & ambrosia (*amrit*) etc.

Sanatan Dharma – the real term for Hindu religion, literally meaning "an everlasting faith" basic features of which are (a) the concept of *karm* (deeds), (b) joint-family system and, (c) caste-system

Sanskars – sacraments for inculcating spiritual grace, imparting benefits to individuals, society and /or environment, there being a total sixteen Hindu *Sanskars* of *Vedic* origin which include several pre-natal *Sanskars* as well as those to be conducted during childhood, later life and after death

Saraswati – the goddess of learning and consort of Lord Brahma

Satyug – 1st of the 4 *Yugas* when righteousness in society was of the highest order

Scriptures – religious literature

Seer – a visionary, typically from the holy fraternity

Self-Cleaning – important early morning ablution quite ritually observed by the Hindus

Shaligram – a manifestation of Lord Vishnu in the form of an ammonite, with the idea of remaining closer to his devotee, *Tulsi*

Shani Dev – the god of evil, evil happenings usually being attributed to him

Shesh Nag – the serpent god providing itself as the reclining couch with its head as canopy, to Lord Vishnu when he relaxes on the ocean surface

Lord Shiva – one among the trinity of Hindu gods as the god of annihilation

Shraadh – a ritual observed by relatives of a dead person in a show of gratitude towards him/her, by offering food to priests, assuming it will go to the dead

Suhag – happy state of married woman whose husband is alive, symbolizing that happy state typically by way of special make-up such as putting red powder on the parting of hair on the head, a red dot on the forehead, etc.

Teerth Sthan – religious place, typically on river bank (*teer*)

Teerthankar – literally meaning 'pathfinder', a title used for the 24 holy teachers of Jain community, who appeared in the past, last and the 24th being Mahavira (599-467 BC), the founder of Jainism

Tilak – a mark on the forehead applied as an auspicious mark, generally using a red powder (*roli*) and putting rice grains on it, symbolic of regeneration – this practice having started during ancient times when mortality rate was high and hence such a sign was considered auspicious

Treta – the 2nd of four *yugas*, the specific and long time period or age during which Lord Rama appeared (for the controversy about *Treta* as the 2nd *yuga*, refer to the details/logic given in the book '*Hindu Gods and Goddesses*' published by Diamond Books which also gives many more interesting details on Hinduism-related facts and myths)

Trimurti – Trinity, literally a group of three but in reference to Hinduism, it is an immense energy, comprising three eternal gods namely Lord Vishnu, Lord Brahma and Lord Shiva

Tulsi – also called *Brinda* or *Vrinda*, believed to be a manifestation of goddess Lakshmi, and a sacred plant (basil) nurtured in Hindu homes, typically outside the threshold

Tulsidas – 16th century poet-saint who scripted *Ramcharit Manas*, the popular Hindi version of Valmiki's *Ramayana*

Upnishads – philosophical discourses documented in scriptures, based on *Vedas*

Vamana – the dwarf as the 5th incarnation of Lord Vishnu who appeared during *Satyug* to restore heavens to gods from Bali who had earlier defeated the gods and captured their heaven

Varaha – the boar as the 3rd incarnation of Lord Vishnu to save earth from destruction caused by demon king Hiranyaksh

Varn – caste-system, a classification among Hindus by caste and a significant feature in Hindu philosophy

Vayu Dev – the *Vedic* god of winds and father of Hanuman of *Ramayana*

Vedanta – philosophy based on *Upnishads* and other *Vedic* literature

Vedas – the oldest and sacred Hindu literature written in Sanskrit language

Vegetarianism – an important element of Hinduism, practice of which imparts purity of mind and body as the foods in this category are primarily *Satvik* (noble) in nature, unlike *Rajasik* foods (spicy foods using lots of clarified butter, condiments etc. aimed at enhancing sensual enjoyment) or *Tamasik* foods (non-vegetarian foods which tend to arouse wild feelings and emotions)

Vikramaditya – the 1st century BC king of Ujjain who founded the *Vikram Era* (starting 58 BC), in celebration of his victory over *Shakas*

Vishnu – Numero uno among gods who protects and the first of the Hindu trinity of eternal gods, others being Lord Brahma and Lord Shiva

Vishwakarma – the celestial architect god, son of Lord Brahma and the originator of the concept of *Vaastu Shastra*– also credited with making of idols of Krishna (as Jagannath) and others at the temple in Puri in Orissa

Yama – the god of Death

Yugas – specific and long time periods or ages in the cosmic time cycle (for details, read *'Hindu Gods & Goddesses'* – Diamond Books)

DIAMOND BOOKS on
Religion & Spirituality

In the common parlance *'Vedas'* means 'knowledge'. These sacred tomes are the beacon lights of enlightenment which dispel the darkness of ignorance from the human minds. In the *Purans,* the story of creation has been delineated in great detail. *Purans* are the timeless tomes of the secrets of the universe and life—about the mysterious dimensions of time and space—about the animate and the inanimate as well as about the flora and the fauna. *Upanishads* are the epitome of eternal knowledge. They form the treasure trove of the sacred *Vedic* philosophy. *Upanishads* are the guiding light of all spiritual knowledge dealing with the universe and life–about creation, birth and death as well as time and space.

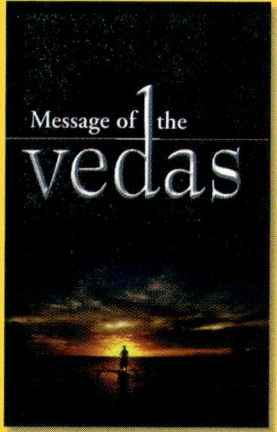

Message of the vedas	 Message of the purans	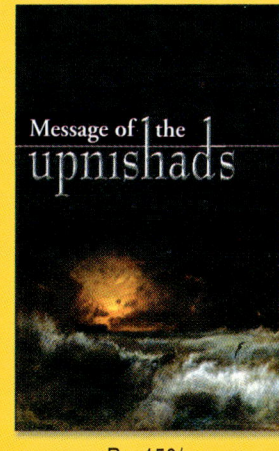 Message of the upnishads	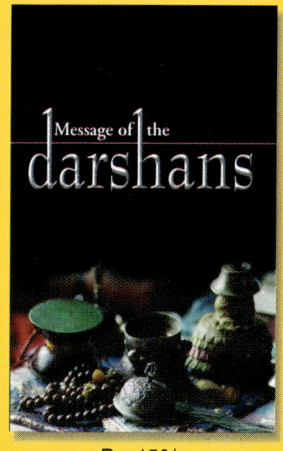 Message of the darshans
Rs. 150/-	Rs. 150/-	Rs. 150/-	Rs. 150/-

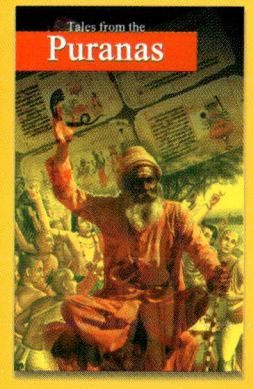

Tales from the Puranas	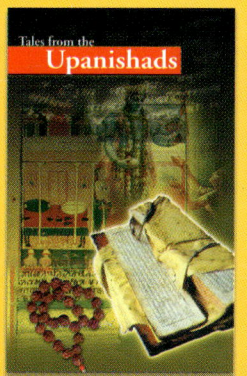 Tales from the Upanishads	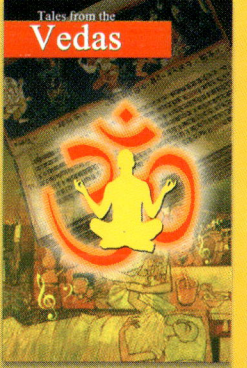 Tales from the Vedas	 Tales from the Mahabharat	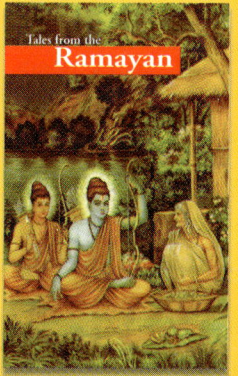 Tales from the Ramayan
Rs. 95/-	Rs. 95/-	Rs. 95/-	Rs. 95/-	Rs. 95/-

DIAMOND BOOKS X-30, Okhla Industrial Area, Phase-II, New Delhi-110020, Ph : 011-41611861, Fax : 011-41611866
E-mail: sales@diamondpublication.com, Website: www.dpb.in

Religion & Spirituality

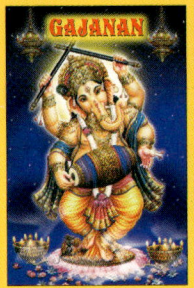

Gajanan	Rs. 95/-
 Neelkanth	Rs. 95/-
Shrimad Bhagavad Gita - Krishna The Chariotter	Rs. 195/-
Lord Rama	Rs. 95/-
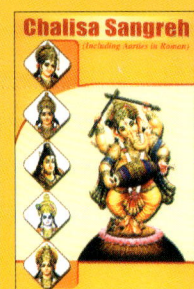 Chalisa Sangreh	Rs. 60/-
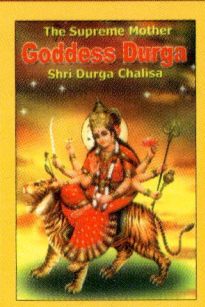 The Supreme Mother Goddess Durga - Shri Durga Chalisa	Rs. 95/-
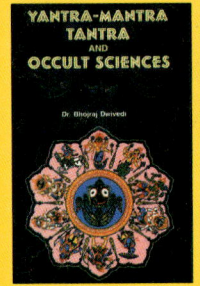 Yantra-Mantra Tantra and Occult Sciences	Rs. 195/-
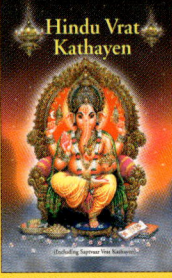 Hindu Vrat Kathayen	Rs. 50/-
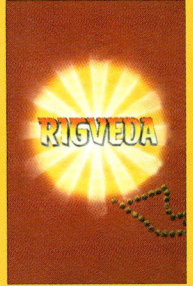 Rigveda	Rs. 95/-
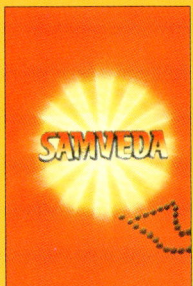 Samveda	Rs. 95/-
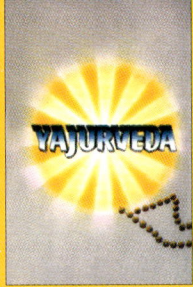 Yajurveda	Rs. 95/-
Atharvaveda	Rs. 95/-
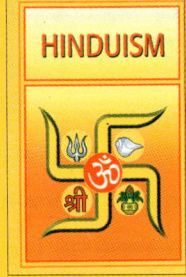 Hinduism	Rs. 125/-
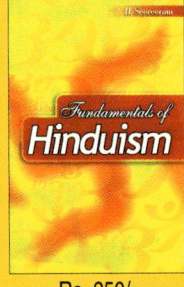 Fundamentals of Hinduism	Rs. 250/-
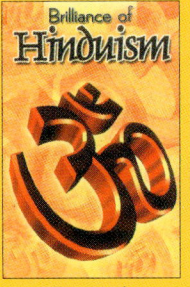 Brilliance of Hinduism	Rs. 125/-
Scientific Bases of Hindu Beliefs	Rs. 95/-
Religious Basis of Hindu Beliefs	Rs. 95/-
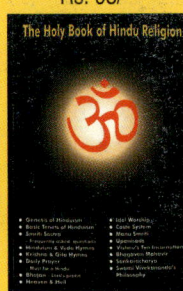 The Holy Book of Hindu Religion	Rs. 100/-
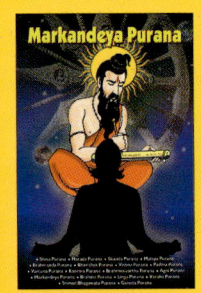 Markandeya Purana	Rs. 75/-
 Brahmvaivartha Purana	Rs. 75/-
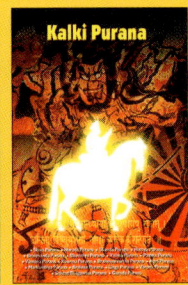 Kalki Purana	Rs. 75/-
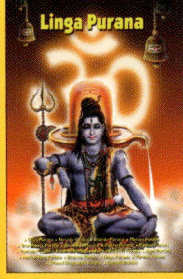 Linga Purana	Rs. 75/-
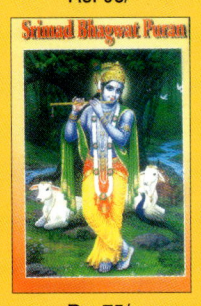 Srimad Bhagwat Puran	Rs. 75/-
 Devi Bhagwat Puran	Rs. 75/-
 Vishnu Purana	Rs. 95/-
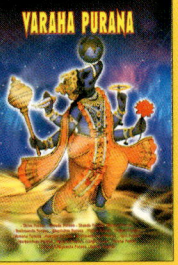 Varaha Purana	Rs. 75/-
 Agni Purana	Rs. 75/-
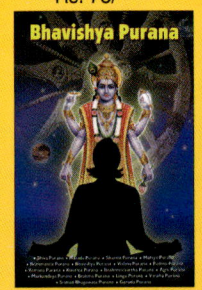 Bhavishya Purana	Rs. 75/-
 Garuda Purana	Rs. 75/-
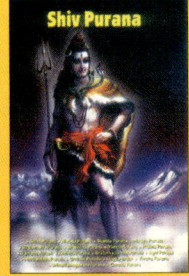 Shiv Purana	Rs. 95/-

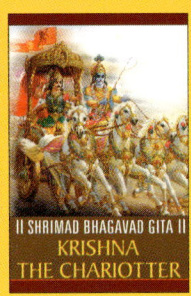

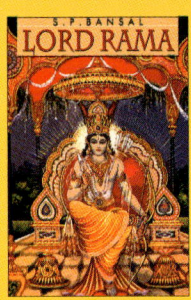

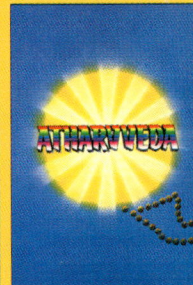

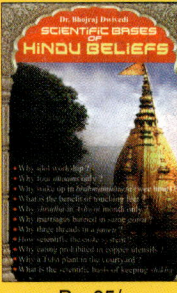

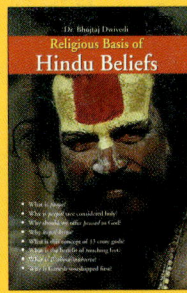

All These Books are Available in Hindi Also.

GAUTAM BUDDHA   Suresh Narain Mathur   Price : Rs. 295/-

This book is an attempt to provide a clear insight into the several interesting and intriguing details on Buddha who is acknowledged as the most significant spiritual light of Asia. The book also provides details on the features of the popular religion of Buddhism, founded by Buddha. Apart from the life of Buddha, this book gives details of Buddha's doctrines in clear graphics for the first time.

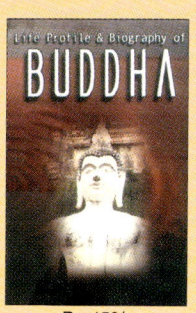

Rs. 150/-

Rs. 150/-

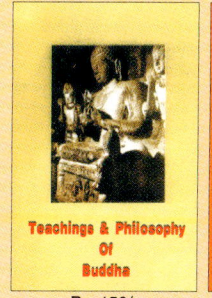

Rs. 150/-

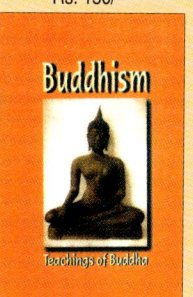

Rs. 150/-

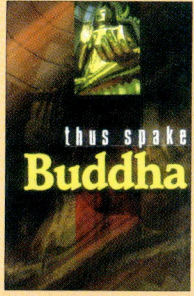

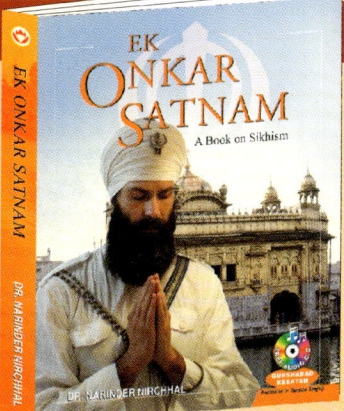

Rs. 150/-

EK ONKAR SATNAM   Dr. Narinder Nirchhal   Price : Rs. 395/-

Sikhism has a theology which is based on the fundamental truth: **'Ek Onkar Satnam'** (oneness of God and the only truth is His name) and on the ethics about honesty and hard work and building a classless and casteless society.

EK ONKAR SATNAM highlights these and other characteristics of the Sikh religion which was founded by Guru Nanak about five centuries ago.

DIAMOND BOOKS
X-30, Okhla Industrial Area, Phase-II, New Delhi-110020, Ph : 011-41611861, Fax : 011-41611866
E-mail: sales@diamondpublication.com, Website: www.dpb.in

HINDU GODS AND GODDESSES

Suresh Narain Mathur, B.K. Chaturvedi

Price : Rs. 295/-

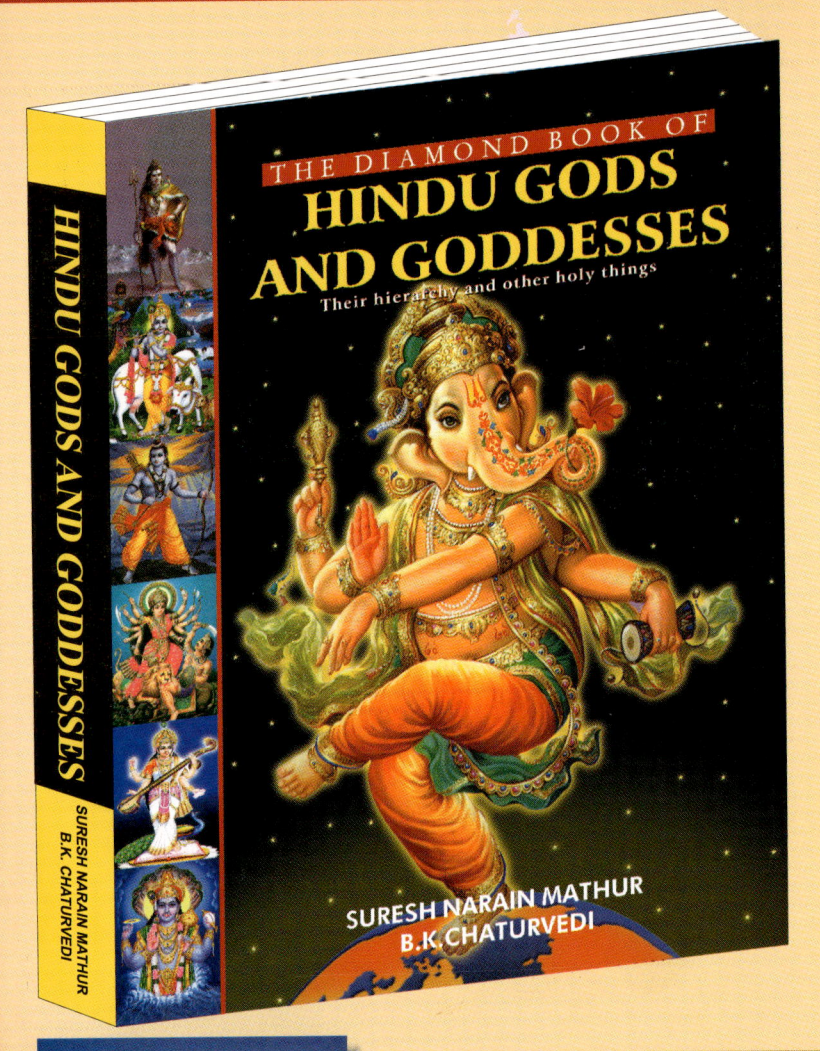

Hindu mythology is the world's richest collection of stories about supernatural personalities and events, both in terms of volume and quality.

HINDU GODS AND GODDESSES– THEIR HIERARCHY AND OTHER HOLY THINGS puts much of the mythological details in a nutshell which can be very informative to the young in general and NRIs in particular.

HIMALAYAN PILGRIMAGE

Pilgrimage to the Himalayas, the legendary *Dev Bhoomi* (the land of gods), traverses temples, sacred mountains and rivers.

HIMALAYAN PILGRIMAGE covers some of the principal and vastly popular religious places such as Mount Kailash, Amarnath, Vaishno Devi and the all-important *Char Dhams* (Yamunotri, Gangotri– the origin of the river Ganges, Kedarnath and Badrinath) which hold promise of salvation, besides offering spectacular landscape in the pristine splendour.

DIAMOND BOOKS X-30, Okhla Industrial Area, Phase-II, New Delhi-110020, Ph : 011-41611861, Fax : 011-41611866
E-mail: sales@diamondpublication.com, Website: www.dpb.in